Victorian Dún Laoghaire

First published 2016

The History Press Ireland
50 City Quay
Dublin 2
Ireland
www.thehistorypress.ie

The History Press Ireland are a member of Publishing Ireland,
the Irish Book Publisher's Association.

British Library Cataloguing in Publication Data.
A catalogue record for this book is available from the British Library.

ISBN 978 1 84588 079 8

Typesetting and origination by The History Press

Contents

PREFACE

I had finished this book when a booklet came to me that, in a few paragraphs, summarises the history of Dún Laoghaire so neatly that I thought it best to repeat those paragraphs here. This 1976 booklet, titled *St. Michael's Hospital, Dún Laoghaire 1878–1976*, is by the late Professor J.B. Lyons and was produced for the centenary of the opening of St Michael's Hospital. In this excerpt he is referring to the period around the opening of the hospital in 1874:

The success of its great harbour assured a prosperous future for Kingstown, but side by side with this prosperity (or rather, hidden behind it) was an insalubrious scene which Dr John Byrne Power (later Medical Superintendent, Kingstown – ed) described:

'On proceeding to examine the township with some care, the first thing that struck me was the number and wretchedness of what I call the slums – miserable courts and rows of wretched hovels, in which a healthy or even decent life is well-nigh impossible. These are, for the most part, hidden from view by dwellings of a more respectable character, being, in many cases, erected in what were formerly the yards or gardens belonging to the houses which conceal them, so that all seems prosperous enough to the casual observer. The number of such hovels and of their inhabitants indicates a proletariate out of all proportion to the possibility of employment in such a town.'

During the years in which the port and the railways were being built there was employment for a great many men. On the completion of the harbour, about 1860, the younger men sought work elsewhere but others remained unemployed.

'Thus Kingstown (Power continues) presents some of the worst features of a town of decaying industry, crumbling hovels, and an undue proportion of perhaps the most helpless class in the community, worn-out workmen, too old to seek employment elsewhere and clinging to the spot which once afforded them the means of comfortable existence. To these conditions we owe our low birth-rate, relatively high death-rate, and large admission to the Union Workhouse.'

I would disagree with Prof. Lyons on one point of detail. He suggests that the wretched conditions in parts of the town date from about 1860. I would suggest that a more appropriate date might be twenty years earlier.

There were two Kingstowns, closely enmeshed and intertwined in the sense that they occupied spaces within metres of each other, but separated in terms of worldly wealth, access to basic necessities of life and opportunity to reach one's potential, with all of the consequences of that separation. In this book, I call them 'Visible Kingstown' and 'Invisible Kingstown'.

Visible Kingstown was a splendid harbour town, a preferred Dublin suburb where many of the city's merchants and professional classes lived. Visible Kingstown can be seen in many photographs of the later Victorian period and its buildings and artefacts can still be seen in the town today.

Invisible Kingstowners lived in conditions of extreme poverty and occupied the backyards, courts, laneways and other hidden cul-de-sacs of the town. They were not often photographed. Their buildings have been demolished. Even the addresses of almost every enclave they occupied have long been obliterated from memory.

This book does not pretend to be a balanced unbiased history of the town. Such a history has been done before. While attempting to give a flavour of Visible Kingstown, it tries to shine some additional light on the Invisible Kingstowners, a very large segment of the population whose situation has not been adequately recorded, and to describe the locations and circumstances in which they lived. In general, it tries not to attribute blame for the extensive problems of poverty in the town, nor does it assign credit to any individual or group who may have alleviated that poverty. Wherever blame is attributed, it is reserved for the Lords of the Soil (in Gaelic the 'Tiarnaí Talún') who, on foot of a very tiny investment made long before the town was developed, reaped an incalculable reward in terms of rents.

Acknowledgements

Three people in particular have made their large private collections available to me in the course of developing this book, and I am immensely grateful to them.

Mick Breen lives in south Wexford. He is an avid collector of early photographic material, including images and associated paraphernalia. His collection of very early CDVs, cabinet photographs, and stereoviews is of national significance. He is a former resident of Dún Laoghaire.

Martha Bernie lives in Los Angeles, California and has distant Irish ancestry. On a trip to Dalkey in 1990, she fell in love with the whole area and has considered it to be her spiritual home ever since. She now comes to Glasthule nearly every year. Her daily blog at https://homethoughtsfromabroad626.wordpress.com has a huge archive of recipes, and of images of Ireland, Missouri and California, interspersed with snippets of history and genealogy. She has a large collection of antique postcards, CDVs and cabinet images as well as a modest collection of antique Irish silver.

Geraldine Manley's roots are deeply embedded in Dún Laoghaire. Her grandfather's bootmaking business at 132 Lower George's Street is listed in *Thom's Directory* from about 1918 onwards. Her family had been collecting local memorabilia well before that date, including concert programmes, sports memorabilia and newspapers. Geraldine is also the founder of the very active (member-only) Facebook site, 'Dún Laoghaire Past and Present'.

In addition I would like to thank Colin Scudds of the Dún Laoghaire Borough Historical Society who has reviewed much of the text and has provided maps of Dún Laoghaire dated 1866 as well as photos. The various publications of the society have been very useful for researching and crosschecking information.

Michael Merrigan and the members of the Genealogical Society of Ireland have been helpful with advice, and with newspaper snippets.

Frances Fletcher has provided photos of her family origins – the only photos I could locate showing life in the poorest parts of Kingstown.

The management of St Michael's Hospital provided access to the original plans of the hospital

Patrick Roche provided the cover photo of workmen at Clarence Street.

Photographs from the Lawrence Collection have been reproduced by kind permission of the National Library of Ireland

Joe Fleming provided the 1900 picture of Upper George's Street showing the demolition for street widening.

I have been a regular user of the Local History Section of the very fine new Lexicon Library at Dún Laoghaire, which has now made its collection more accessible.

The massively improved online digital access to history and genealogical resources has been immeasurably helpful in researching, assembling, and crosschecking information.

The Pictorium, Monkstown Farm has provided restoration services for some of the oldest photos.

There is nothing like good family support in a project such as this. My daughter, Julie Davis (*née* Conlon), has done meticulous work on improving the text, including reminding me of the distinctions between the words 'sewer', 'sewage' and 'sewerage'. I want to thank my angel wife, Gabrielle, for her constant love, support, encouragement at all times.

Every effort has been made to trace owners of copyright material and we hope that no copyright has been infringed. Pardon is sought and apology is made if the contrary is the case, and a correction will be made in future editions of this book.

The vastly improved online digital access to history and genealogical resources has been immeasurably helpful in researching, assembling, and cross-checking information:

Item	Website Publisher	Website
Maps (contemporary, *c.* 1904 and *c.* 1860)	Ordnance Survey Ireland	www.osi.ie
Censuses (1901 and 1911)	National Archives of Ireland	www.census.nationalarchives.ie
Griffiths Valuation books and maps	OMS Services Ltd, Eneclann Ltd and the National Library of Ireland.	www.askaboutireland.ie/griffith-valuation
Newspaper Archives	Irish Newspaper Archives Ltd	www.irishnewsarchive.com
Thom's Directories 1850 & 1852	Google Inc.	https://books.google.com
Enhanced British Parliamentary Papers on Ireland	Dippam	www.dippam.ac.uk/eppi
Irish Statute Books (pre-1922 Acts)	Office of the Attorney General	www.irishstatutebook.ie

The publication of this book has been assisted by funding from:

Dún Laoghaire Rathdown County Council • Genealogical Society of Ireland • Dún Laoghaire Borough Historical Society

Dún Laoghaire
Borough
Historical
Society

From a Fishing Village to a Major Victorian Town

EARLY DUNLEARY

In the early eighteenth century, Dunleary or Dunlary is shown on maps as a remote, tiny hamlet on a protrusion of rock overlooking a cove and river mouth. This original village was close to the location where the Purty Kitchen bar and restaurant now stands. Virtually all traces of that original village were removed in the construction of the harbour and the railway. It was a remote settlement with few habitations around it and no real road to the village.

At that time, the water of Dunleary harbour came up to the back of what is now Synnott Terrace, Cumberland Street, Dunleary Hill, Longford Place, and the Salthill end of the area known as Old Dunleary. The areas now occupied by the Purty Kitchen, the West Pier Service Station, the Clearwater Cove Apartments, the West Pier Business Campus, and parts of the railway and road would then have been under water at high tide.

According to Francis Erlington Ball's *A History of County Dublin* (Alex Thom and Co., 1902):

> Though less fashionable than Newtown Castle Byrne, Dunleary was then a seaside place of amusement. Swift, writing in 1721 to his sub-Dean, asks him how often he had been with his wife to Dunleary, and about the same time some verses appeared, which invited the ladies of Dublin to repair in coach or on car to Dunleary, where they would find honest residents and could procure good ale. Such luxuries as meat and wine they were recommended to bring with them. Dunleary was also possessed of at least one good dwelling, known as the Great House. In it probably died, in 1711, Lady Mary Sheares, of Dunleary, daughter of Richard, second Earl of Barrymore, and wife, first of the Rev. Gerald Barry, and secondly, of the Rev. Christopher Sheares, of Tandragee, and in it resided, successively, Lord Tullamore, afterwards Earl of Charleville; Lord Southwell, and Viscount Lanesborough. Later on Mr. John Garden, ancestor of the Gardens of Fishmoyne, leased a large place near Dunleary, which comprised lands known as the Seafield, the Rockfield, and the Towerfield, and which was bounded on one side by the sea, and on the other by the high road from Monkstown to Bullock.

In the 1760s, a harbour wall was built outwards on the east side of the existing river mouth, and this harbour wall is now incorporated into the main harbour as the 'Coal Quay'. It provided a better opportunity to land fish and was used on occasions for vessels travelling to and from the various Welsh ports.

Corrig Castle stood alone about 1km (½ mile) east of the village, located at the top of Northumberland Avenue. It was an unusual house with battlements and is reputed to have provided refuge to King James II before his departure from Ireland in 1690. It was demolished about 1936.

LORDS OF THE SOIL

Dunleary was still a small village when leases were created in relation to the lands upon which the town was later built. East of the then village, the area where most of the town of Dún Laoghaire now stands was open ground all the way from the coast to Glenageary. With the exception of a couple of houses, the area was unfenced land and was unsuitable for any farming activity other than sheep grazing. It was strewn with boulders, and rocky outcrops betrayed the presence of granite deposits beneath the surface in some areas. The landlords of the time, Lords Longford and de Vesci, could not have foreseen how valuable those lands would soon become. The leases, dated about 1803, gave them a rental stream that lasted initially for ninety-nine years and were renewed to provide a further rental stream through the twentieth century. Through the years, a structure of leases and sub-leases was developed which formed the title to every place in the town and led to a structure of rents paid by occupiers of premises and lands to sub-lease holders who in turn paid rents to the lords.

The title 'Lords of the Soil', although sometimes used in relation to certain other landlords elsewhere, became particularly associated with these two lords, and was used by themselves and their agents from time to time. For many people in Kingstown and Dún Laoghaire, they were hate figures, but their baronial names (Longford, de Vesci, and Knapton) as well as their family names (Pakenham and Vesey) live on in the names of local roads.

MARTELLO TOWERS

At each end of the open area where the town was later built, Martello towers were erected for coastal defence purposes in the first decade of the nineteenth century. One tower was located in the vicinity of Battery Bridge, Crofton Road, coincidentally on or near the reputed site of the original fort (dún). That tower was removed about 1836 when the original (1834) Dublin–Kingstown railway was extended into the town. The other tower was located in a rocky area to the east of the town. The area around the tower was quarried from about 1817 for the construction of the harbour. The tower is clearly shown at the quarry edge on maps of the 1850s but the extended quarry is shown on maps of the 1870s and the tower is missing. The abandoned quarry was filled in 1890 to create the People's Park. The location of that tower was close to the Summerhill gate of the park.

ERECTING THE HARBOUR

By 1815, Dunleary had developed from a few houses to a fishing village centred around the small harbour, with houses along what is now Cumberland Street and where Cumberland Street meets Clarence Street and York Road.

On 11 July 1815, the Westminster government, in a single-page document, passed 'An Act to authorise the Appointment of Commissioners for erecting a Harbour for Ships to the Eastward of Dunleary, within the Port and Harbour of Dublin' (CAP.CXCL). The harbour, and the town which grew around it, were soon to be called Kingstown, and later Dún Laoghaire.

The legislation had followed a lengthy campaign. The campaign was for an 'Asylum Harbour'. An asylum harbour is a place where ships can take refuge in stormy weather. Such a harbour was considered as necessary because of the dangers associated with entering Dublin Bay at the time. One such harbour was built at Howth in the early 1800s but it proved unsatisfactory. The campaign for Dunleary followed a series of maritime disasters, the most significant of which happened on the night of 18 November 1807, when about 400 lives were lost from two ships which floundered in the vicinity of Monkstown and Blackrock. This campaign was initiated by Captain Richard Toutcher, a Scandinavian-born seaman, and it was he who first selected the location for the asylum harbour on account of its depth of water and sound bottom. He may have had access to the report of John Rennie, the great engineer of harbours who visited the area in 1802.

The concept of an asylum harbour is simple: just enclose an area of deep water behind a stout wall, leaving an opening sufficiently large to allow ships to enter, but arranged so that the effects of wind and wave on the enclosed water are minimised. The enclosed water is therefore safe in times of storm. In design terms, it is quite different from a trading harbour, which is designed with quaysides and facilities for the efficient loading, unloading and carriage of large quantities of goods.

The appointment of commissioners enabled the planning of the project to commence but did not set aside any funding for the construction of the harbour. The commissioners set to work very quickly. Within a year, they had a plan. Their plan was for a single pier projecting northward from the land, slightly east of the position of the present East Pier, and with a shape quite similar to that East Pier. This pier would act as a breakwater. In eleven months they brought forward plans to the point where the government could commit, on 20 June 1816, to the construction of the harbour in 'An Act for erecting an Harbour for ships to the Eastward of Dunleary, within the Port of Dublin'. This act facilitated the funding and much of the legislative support required to build the harbour.

Before the construction of the harbour commenced in 1817, the plan was modified and expanded to create a second pier. John Rennie's modified plan was indeed for an asylum harbour in the true sense of the term. It would have stout walls enclosing 101 hectares (251 acres) of water. The seaward sides of the walls had a shallow incline, which was designed to break the waves. The inward side of the walls had a steep incline but was not vertical. The walls were not designed for ships to moor alongside. The eventual design of the pier heads left an entrance of about 230m (760ft). Rennie was an experienced designer of major engineering projects. He had designed numerous lighthouses, canals and bridges throughout the kingdom, and was responsible for many of the world's largest docks and harbours, including those at Plymouth, Liverpool and Hull as well as the East India and West India docks in London.

The harbour project would be an astonishing engineering achievement. It would require the construction of massive stout stonewalls outwards from the land into open seas. Foundations beneath those walls would be many times the size of the visible walls and would require extra strength on the seaward side.

Vast quantities of stone of the highest quality would be required in the construction of the harbour. Railroads for horse-drawn carts were laid to local quarries and to quarries at Bullock and Dalkey. The Dalkey railroad included a funicular arrangement to bring carts down the hillside section of the track to Barnhill Road, and from there onwards the carts would be pulled by horses. It became known as 'The Metals'. Over a million tonnes of stone was moved by those horse-drawn railcarts over the following few years.

Mention must be made of the extraordinary action of the aforementioned Richard Toutcher, who, in anticipation of the construction of the harbour, at his own expense, secured the rights to quarry stone at Dalkey, and presented those rights to the harbour builders free-of-charge.

DEVELOPING THE NEW TOWN

It was immediately recognised that a town of some significance would develop in the area. A few straight lines drawn on a map of this area became the layout for the new town. These lines are clearly shown on maps and plans of 1817. Up to that point, most towns in Ireland had developed along roads which were originally laid out to follow the boundaries of farms, but this new town with straight streets had a layout which was almost unique in Ireland. The main street, referred to as 'High Street' on one early map, and later renamed George's Street, was an absolutely straight line, which ran from the original village for more than a mile in a south-easterly direction. It was set out as just wide enough for two carriages to meet, with a footpath which initially was only on one side. The roads, which were later to become Marine Road, Lower Glenageary Road and Park Road, are all shown on these 1817 plans.

George's Street quickly became a mixed-use street. It soon had a wide range of shops and services. It also had whole sections devoted to private housing. Some of these houses were demolished over 100 years ago, but some fine houses still remain, particularly on the north side of Upper George's Street. *Pettigrew and Olson's Directory* of 1834 lists about 120 businesses operating on George's Street, including a wide range of retailers, trades, and professions. Among the services on the street were those of a straw bonnetmaker, tinplate worker, stay and corset maker, measurer, nailer, cooper, tallow chandler, surgeon, and accoucheur (a male midwife).

The construction of the harbour immediately attracted a workforce which at times is said to have exceeded 1,000. Some were casual labourers and many were unskilled. There are reports that initially tented villages were used as their accommodation. But a labour force of that size, many with families, creates a need for housing. It also creates secondary employment in supply and support services, and so the town developed very rapidly.

Within two years, the transformation of Dunleary was well under way. *The History of the City of Dublin* (by Warburton, Whitelaw and Walsh, published in 1818 by Cadell and Davies) describes the early development of the area:

From the speculation of this pier, and the benefit it is likely to confer on the vicinity, the value of every thing is highly encreased, and the village from being the inconsiderable and dirty abode of a few fishermen, in the bottom of a valley, has now extended itself along the cliffs in every direction. Dunleary was therefore the last residence in this direction, the country lying between it and Bullock presented a sterile solitary tract covered with furze and heath, without road or inclosure, and passable only by a few paths. Within ten years, the aspect of the country has been changed; it is pierced by good roads in all directions, fields are enclosed and reclaimed, and the whole space is covered over with neat and even elegant villas, built of hewn mountain granite. From the pure air, dry soil and bold coast of this tract, it is now preferred as a summer residence to the sandy shore of the interior of the bay.

Construction of the harbour continued for many years. In August 1821, the harbour was sufficiently advanced for the King to visit and rename it the 'Royal Harbour of George IV'. He took the opportunity to change the name of the town to 'King's Town', which was quickly dropped in favour of Kingstown. The name Kingstown remained for about 100 years.

Less well known is the extent to which the streets of the town were also named after members of the King's direct family.

1 George's Street is named after the king himself
2 Sussex Street after his brother Augustus, the Earl of Sussex
3 Clarence Street after his brother William (later King William IV), the Earl of Clarence
4 Cumberland Street after his brother Ernest Augustus (later Ernest Augustus, King of Hanover), the Earl of Cumberland
5 York Street (later renamed York Road) after his brother Frederick, the Duke of York
6 Cambridge Terrace after his brother Adolphus, the Earl of Cambridge
7 Adelaide Street after Adelaide, the wife of his brother William. Adelaide later became queen consort to King William IV

In the 1860s, the harbour was considered completed and the cost of construction up to that date was estimated at £1 million.

CONNECTING THE TOWN

The Kingstown–Holyhead/Liverpool mail service was introduced in 1826. No consideration had been given during the construction of the harbour to the provision of this service and there were no appropriate docking positions. A short wooden wharf was constructed close to where the bandstand now stands on the East Pier. This service was operated by paddle steamers owned by the government.

Soon afterwards, a proposal was considered to build a canal from Dublin through to Kingstown, thereby creating the opportunity for ships to bypass the treacherous mouth of the river Liffey when coming into Dublin. A number of possible designs were considered and recommended, but despite support from wealthy and influential individuals, the canal was never developed.

The coming of the railway to Kingstown in 1834 added a huge impetus to the development of the town. The railway was conceived as a commuter line. It would have regular services to and from Westland Row in Dublin throughout the day. As well as providing a service for local commuters, it provided convenience to passengers from Dublin intending to travel on the mail service ships to Britain.

Contemporary descriptions of the town depict it as being a bit haphazard and even shabby. This would suggest that some of the early buildings were built to a poor standard, and poorly maintained. In his *Irish Sketch Book* (1842), William Makepeace Thackeray, poet, novelist, and travel writer wrote:

Numerous terraces and pleasure-houses have been built in the place – they stretch row after row along the banks of the sea and rise one above another on the hill. The rents of these houses are said to be high; the Dublin citizens crowd into them in Summer; and a great source of pleasure and comfort must it be to them to have the fresh sea breezes and prospects so near to the metropolis.

The better sort of houses are handsome and spacious; but the fashionable quarter is yet in an unfinished state, for enterprising architects are always beginning new roads, rows and terraces; nor are those already built by any means complete. Beside the aristocratic part of the town is a commercial one, and nearer to Dublin stretch lines of low cottages which have not a Kingstown look at all, but are evidently of the Dunleary

period … The houses have a battered, rakish look and seem going to ruin before their time. After the town come the suburbs of pleasure-houses; low, one-storeyed cottages for the most part; some neat and fresh, some that have passed away from the genteel state altogether and exhibit downright poverty; some in a state of transition, with broken windows and pretty romantic names upon tumble-down gates.

From 1850, the mail boat service was operated by the City of Dublin Steam Packet Company and from 1859 the railway and the mail boat were fully connected. Services were scheduled to match the sailings and to deliver passengers directly to the quayside on the newly constructed Carlisle Pier.

A MISSED OPPORTUNITY?

A town with a large harbour, a railway connection to the capital city and a location that made it the shortest route across the Irish Sea might have been expected to develop into a major port for the import and export of cargo. In addition, Dublin port was a treacherous place for shipping and its dangers had indeed been the rationale for the construction of Kingstown Harbour.

But Kingstown was never really designed for cargo. It was essentially an asylum port, designed for shelter. It was designed for the benefit of Dublin port. The harbour walls were not designed for the unloading of ships. Berth facilities were not considered in the original development of the harbour, and when they were constructed, they were designed primarily for postal and passenger services.

Similarly, the railway was not designed for the movement of goods. It was essentially a passenger commuter service. The city terminus of the railway at Westland Row was not connected to any other part of the rail network. The frequency of passenger trains on the line meant that there was little capacity for goods services. In 1866, plans were made to extend the railway line northwards by means of a tunnel that would connect it to the other rail lines of the country. The same proposal would have enhanced the West Pier for commercial trading. Plans for the tunnel were developed by Messrs Mallet and Burke. Initial borings for the tunnel were commenced under the direction of Mr Matthew E. Talbot as chief engineer, and permanent shafts were sunk on both sides of the river to the full depth of the proposed tunnel. However, the project appears to have fizzled out. It was not until 1891 that the loop-line bridge across the Liffey was built to make the necessary rail connections to the other railway stations of Dublin, and thereby to the national rail network.

Within Kingstown itself, rails were laid along the Victoria Wharf and the Trader's Wharf for use by goods trains, but their use appears to have been limited. No large cranes or other facilities for unloading large cargoes were ever installed on the wharfs.

Coal for local use was imported through Kingstown throughout the Victorian period – and the very large number of chimneys on the older houses in Kingstown suggests that the amount used by each household was substantial – but the demand did not require large facilities and did not provide a lot of local jobs.

It is interesting to speculate how history might have been different if the instructions given to John Rennie as lead designer of the harbour included a few extra words. If the harbour had been designed for trading, or even if it had later been adapted for trading, Dún Laoghaire might have developed in quite a different way. Tilbury in England became a major port because of its strategic location in relation to London. With its equally strategic location, Dún Laoghaire might have developed into the largest port in Ireland. Newtownsmith would likely have been extended outwards into Scotsman's Bay and would nowadays be stacked high with containers. The East Pier and West Pier would be lined with cranes. The M50 would be connected to Queen's Road by a tunnel and the railway would be six tracks wide. Many of today's residents would be horrified to consider such an outcome.

THE RETAIL TOWN DEVELOPS

The Industrial Revolution never really reached Kingstown. It became mainly a town of retailers and service providers, and these were almost entirely located along George's Street, Cumberland Street, Clarence Street, and York Street (later renamed York Road). When Queen Victoria ascended to the throne in 1837, there was a full range of shops offering food, clothes, alcohol, and the other essentials of life.

By the end of Queen Victoria's reign, the streets of Kingstown, and most particularly George's Street Upper and Lower, were probably the most cosmopolitan streets in Ireland and matched some of the best in Britain. The town had all of the normal day-to-day foods and clothing shops, but also had a wide range of specialist shops of all types. There seems to have been a specialist shop for each and every type of food. There were flour shops, fruit shops, tea merchants, coffee shops, Italian food shops, poulterers, dairies, pork butchers, fishmongers, and bakeries. Indeed, one could go to Findlaters who sold all of the above under a single roof. One could sip coffee in the Kingstown Coffee Palace near St Michael's Hospital or have ice cream in one of the cafés where the shopping centre is now located.

QUEEN VICTORIA COMES TO KINGSTOWN

In the twilight years of her reign, Queen Victoria came to Dublin by way of Kingstown. It was her third time passing through the harbour. She disembarked at 11.25 a.m. on 4 April 1900, received a welcome address and a bouquet of flowers, and departed by way of Crofton Road at 11.33, bypassing the town centre which had been decorated in her honour. The coast road from the Battery Bridge to the Purty Kitchen had not yet been built so she proceeded along Clarence Street and Cumberland Street. Neither streets were elegant at that time, so she never saw the town at its best.

DUNLEARY/KINGSTOWN TIMELINE

This timeline attempts to give a flavour of some of the important events in the history of Dunleary/Kingstown through the years as well as some of the trivial but interesting events. It covers the period up to the end of the Victorian era and a little bit beyond.

480

Reputed date of the 'Dún' (fort) of Laoghaire

The name Dún Laoghaire translates as Laoghaire's Fort and relates to a fifth-century 'High King' of Ireland whose main base was at Tara in County Meath, 30 miles north-west of Dublin. There is no written evidence of a fort of Laoghaire in or near the town, nor have any reliably authenticated artefacts from that period been found in the area. The reputed location of the fort is in the area of the railway bridge, close to the original (1767) harbour, now known as the Coal Quay. That particular location has been the subject of many transformations, including:

The construction of the original harbour in 1767

The construction of a Martello tower and gun battery about 1806

The demolition of the Martello tower and the construction of the railway line and bridge about 1837

The rebuilding of the bridge and the modification of the railway for electrification in 1984

As a result of these activities, it is unlikely that any further archaeological evidence of the origins of the town will be found at this location.

1756

Dunlary village and its coffee house
are shown on John Rocque's map.
This is not necessarily the first
map to show the tiny village,
but it is certainly the most
significant map of the period.

1716

Dean Jonathan Swift sailed
from Dunlary and wrote
a letter from Chester
confirming his safe arrival
on 2 September. Writing
in 1721, he strongly
recommended Dunlary
as a watering hole.

Arthur Young, in his
book *A Tour of Ireland,
1776–1779*, opens with
the fact that on 19 June,
he sailed from Holyhead
in the packet *Claremont*.
'After a tedious passage
of twenty two hours,
landed on the 20th in the
morning at Dunlary.'

1767 — 1776

1710

Monkstown, Bullock, Dalkey,
and Killiney are all shown on maps
by Frederik De Wit and others of
the period but there is no reference
to Dunleary. This may be explained by
the fact that Dunleary had no castle.

Construction of Dunleary Harbour,
supervised by Charles Vallancey

The harbour of Dunleary built in 1767 is attributed to Thomas Eyre,
who died in 1772, and Charles Vallancey (1721-1812), who was a military
engineer posted to Ireland and assigned the title, Surveyor General of Ireland.

Dunleary harbour, at that time, came up close to the back of what is now
Synnott Terrace, Cumberland Street, Dunleary Hill, Longford Place, and the
Salthill end of the area known as Old Dunleary. The areas now occupied
by the Purty Kitchen, the West Pier Service Station, the Clearwater Cove
Apartments, the West Pier Business Campus (possibly), the former Wallace's
coalyard, and parts of the railway would then have been under water at
high tide. The harbour was flanked on its eastern side by a harbour wall
that is now incorporated into the main harbour as the 'Coal Quay'.

The harbour wall is depicted on some maps as having an ornamented
end. The village of Dunleary or Dunlary consisted of a small number
of houses and a coffee house overlooking the harbour. The low status
of the town at that time can be gauged from the fact that no road
to Dunleary is depicted on contemporary maps of the period.

The area now occupied by the town is shown as a rocky
commonage leading to a rocky shoreline.

1804

Ninety-nine-year leases commenced for the Longford and de Vesci estates on which much of the town was built.

Construction of the Martello towers at Glasthule and Dunleary commenced. The location of the Glasthule tower, long demolished, is just inside the eastern end perimeter of the People's Park. The location of the Dunleary tower appears to have been in front of the present-day Bord Iascaigh Mhara (BIM) building, close to the railway bridge known as Battery Bridge.

1802

John Rennie, who eventually designed the harbour, visited Dunleary. He assembled a proposal for the development of a ship canal that would join the city to the tiny harbour in Dunleary. The plan was not progressed at this time. However, it was resurrected almost thirty years later, when much of the Kingstown harbour had been built. The plan divided opinion and was shelved after much debate.

1799

Much of the land where Dún Laoghaire now stands came into the possession of Lords Longford and De Vesci.

1800

Survey of Dunleary Harbour by Captain William Bligh

Before the construction of the North Wall and South Wall in Dublin, the profile of Dublin Bay made it difficult for shipping. Much of the problem was attributed to moving sandbars. Captain William Bligh (1754-1817) was commissioned to advise. Bligh had previously been commanding lieutenant of the HMS *Bounty* during the infamous mutiny. In relation to Dunleary harbour, Bligh stated, 'It has nothing to recommend it, being ill adapted for its purpose and ill taken care of, and although sheltered from the east winds, is much incommoded by the swell which sets in around the pier end as well as with the northerly winds.'

Bligh's survey found the harbour to be 149m (163 yards) long and with a high-tide depth of 4.2m (14ft).

Sinking of HMS *Prince of Wales* and *Rochdale*

Dublin Bay is littered with the wrecks of ships but none had so dramatic
an impact as the sinking of HMS *Prince of Wales* and the *Rochdale*.
Both vessels sank on the same night, 19 November 1807.

HMS *Prince of Wales* was a sloop of 104 tonnes (103 tons). It was carrying over
120 soldiers when it was driven on to the rocks at Blackrock. The captain
and some crew survived but most of the soldiers were drowned.

The *Rochdale* was a brig of 137 tonnes (135 tons). 265 lives were lost when she went
on the rocks at Seapoint, Monkstown, less than a mile west of the village of Dunleary.

The deceased were buried in mass graves at Carrickbrennan cemetery and
at Belle Vue cemetery on the Merrion Road, near the Tara Towers hotel.

A campaign for the development of an asylum harbour in the vicinity
of Dublin began almost immediately. Scandinavian-born former ship's
captain, Richard Toutcher (1758–1851) specifically promoted the
case for the construction of the asylum harbour at Dunleary.

On 11 July 1815, the Westminster
government, in a single-page
document, passed 'An Act to authorise
the Appointment of Commissioners
for erecting an Harbour for Ships
to the Eastward of Dunleary, within
the Port and Harbour of Dublin'
(CAP.CXCL) and the Commissioners
set to work very quickly.

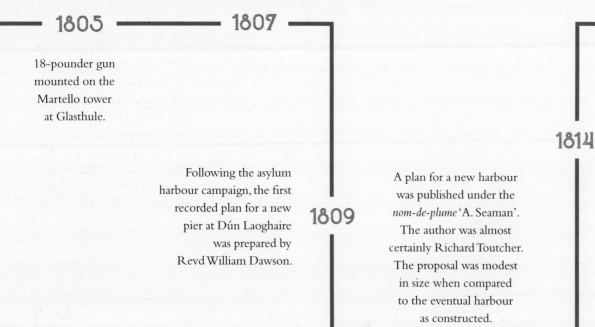

1805 — **1807**

18-pounder gun
mounted on the
Martello tower
at Glasthule.

Following the asylum
harbour campaign, the first
recorded plan for a new
pier at Dún Laoghaire
was prepared by
Revd William Dawson.

1809

A plan for a new harbour
was published under the
nom-de-plume 'A. Seaman'.
The author was almost
certainly Richard Toutcher.
The proposal was modest
in size when compared
to the eventual harbour
as constructed.

1811

1814

1815

Richard Toutcher acquired
quarrying rights at Dalkey Quarry
at his own expense. He presented
those rights later to the Harbour
Commissioners free of charge.

The Commissioners had advanced plans to the point where the government could commit, on 20 June 1816, to the construction of the harbour in 'An Act for erecting an Harbour for ships to the Eastward of Dunleary, within the Port of Dublin'. The plan was to construct a single pier.

1816

Lieutenant William Hutchinson (1793-1881) was appointed as first Harbourmaster.

On 6 June, the lighthouse on the East Pier was lit. 'The light to be exhibited will be of a bright colour, on the revolving principle, and will attain its greatest magnitude once in every minute'.

1822

The George IV obelisk, constructed on an outcrop of granite on Harbour Road, later renamed as Queen's Road, was unveiled. The name of Richard Toutcher was omitted and Toutcher's contribution to the harbour project was never adequately recognised.

1823

1824

The plan was modified and a second pier was added to the plan by John Rennie, chief engineer.

The Dunleary harbour foundation stone was laid by Earl Whitworth, Lord-Lieutenant.

1817

King George IV visited Ireland. He departed from the harbour, which he renamed to 'The Royal Harbour of George IV'. He renamed the town as King's Town, which was soon shortened to Kingstown. The town was known by this name for almost 100 years.

John Rennie, chief engineer of the harbour, died. His son, John Rennie Junior, continued his father's work.

1821

The hulk *Essex* moored in Kingstown as a convict ship, mainly holding convicts awaiting deportation. It continued until about 1837.

1825

The 'Bill for enlarging Powers of Commissioners for erecting Harbour for Ships to eastward of Dunleary (Kingstown) in Port of Dublin' passed in Westminster.

1826

The first service in St Michael's Roman Catholic church was recorded though the building was not finished until 1835.

1827

A brief Account of the Diseases that appeared on board the Essex Prison Hulk, during the Years 1825, 26, and 27 was published by John Speer, a medical doctor and a surgeon in the Royal Navy.

1828

The first Kingstown regatta was held.

James Crofton died. He was a builder and the first harbour commissioner.

Scot's church, a Presbyterian church, opened on York Road. The building later became Kingstown Grammar School when the new Presbyterian church was built across the road.

1829

Kingstown Roman Catholic parish was established. Revd Bartholomew Sheridan was appointed as first parish priest.

1831

The population of Kingstown was recorded as 5,736.

There was a cholera outbreak in Kingstown. It lasted into the following year.

'An Act for Maintaining a Railroad from Westland Row in the City of Dublin to the Head of the Western Pier of the Royal Harbour in the County of Dublin, with Branches to communicate therewith' was passed at Westminster.

The Kingstown Dispensary opened in Kingstown Avenue, now Patrick Street.

Hayes' Royal Hotel, later incorporated into the right-hand end of the Royal Marine, and Kelly's Royal Harbour Hotel opened. Kelly's was at George's Place and was owned by Thomas Kelly and his wife. This name lives on in the nearby Kelly's Avenue.

1834

The Findlater's Irish and Scotch Whiskey Store opened.

The Kingstown Town Commissioners (KTC) were established under 'An Act for the paving, watching, lighting, regulating and otherwise improving the town of Kingstown'. The first KTC meeting was held in Kelly's Royal Hotel in George's Place.

On 17 November, the Dublin to Kingstown railway carried its first passengers. It had eight carriages, drawn by the locomotive *Hibernia*. The terminus was close to the current position of the West Pier service station in Old Dunleary. The track mounting arrangements on granite blocks were soon found to be unsatisfactory and the track was re-laid with wooden sleepers.

The 'Bill to amend Acts relating to Harbour of Kingstown' passed.

The Wesleyan Methodist church on Northumberland Avenue opened. It was rebuilt in 1904.

The railway terminus moved from Old Dunleary to the position of the present-day station.

The Harbour Commissioners were empowered to establish a force of harbour constables.

A report on the convict hulk *Essex* stated that 'a worst form of prison could scarcely be devised'. The convicts were transferred to land-based prisons.

The Anglesea Arms Hotel opened on Crofton Road.

The Quakers commenced construction on the Friends' Meeting Hall. It was extended in 1837 and again in 1880.

1832

The report of the 'select committee appointed to inquire into the expediency and practicability of constructing a ship canal between the City of Dublin and the asylum harbour at Kingstown' recommended that the Dublin to Kingstown Ship Canal project should proceed to undertake a full survey.

Attempts to extend the Dublin–Kingstown railway to Dalkey were stopped by Thomas Gresham.

1833

1836

The Sisters of Mercy established a convent at Sussex Place. This was the second convent for the order, which had been established eight years earlier in Baggot Street, Dublin.

It is believed that the Martello tower at Battery Bridge was demolished at this time.

1835

Victoria Wharf was built and named in honour of the newly crowned queen. Victoria Wharf is now covered over by the car park and roads around the ferry terminal.

The Protestant Episcopal Mariners' church at Kingstown Harbour was opened at Haigh Terrace. It was a simple construction with little ornamentation and no spire. A spire and many other modifications were added in the 1860s. This church was later converted to the National Maritime Museum.

The Quakers extended the Friends' Meeting Hall, in Monkstown, to accommodate increased numbers.

The convict hulk *Essex*, which had been moored in the harbour for thirteen years, was sold for £2,000.

The Dublin to Kingstown railway was re-laid and extended into the position of the present railway station.

1840

The Kingstown Market at Sussex Street opened. It closed about 1860.

Harbourmaster's House, later Moran House, now The Gallery in the grounds of Dún Laoghaire Rathdown Lexicon, was completed. William Hutchinson, Harbourmaster, moved into it.

1841

The population of Kingstown was recorded as 7,229.

On 14 April, Captain Richard Toutcher, who inspired the construction of the harbour, died. He was bankrupt.

1839

1842

The East Pier Lighthouse was completed.

A contract was signed for the construction of the railway station. John Skipton Mulvany was the architect and Roberts was the builder.

1838

The Royal Irish Yacht Club was formed. This club was soon dissolved and became The Kingstown Boat Club. It became the Royal Yacht Club in 1845 and the Royal Saint George Yacht Club in 1847.

George's Street was divided into Lower George's Street and Upper George's Street.

The value of the asylum harbour was proven beyond doubt on 'The Night of the Big Wind', 6–7 January 1839. In one of the worst storms recorded in Ireland, little or no damage was done to shipping in the harbour.

1839

1847

The East Pier Lighthouse opened.

Saint Mary's Convent, a Dominican order, opened. The secondary school closed in 1991 and the site is now occupied by Bloomfield's Shopping Centre.

1848

The Kingstown Cricket Club opened beside Sandycove railway station.

A kitchen was established by the Quakers at the Friends' Meeting House in Monkstown to provide relief to hungry famine victims.

Lady Margaret Huggins (*née* Murray) was born. She spent many of her formative years at 23 Longford Terrace, Monkstown. She specialised in spectroscopy, a branch of astronomy, and made many significant advances in astrophysics in collaboration with her husband.

1843

The Royal Saint George Yacht Club's first clubhouse was completed. John Skipton Mulvany was the architect and Masterson was the builder.

The Kingstown to Dalkey atmospheric railway officially opened 29 March after trials. The train was powered by a stationary vacuum pump located close to Barnhill Road. A vacuum pipe lain between the tracks pulled a piston that was attached to the train.

1846

The County Dublin (Monkstown) Archers was formed. The club later became the Monkstown Archery and Tennis Club in 1877. This was the first tennis club in Ireland.

1844

The Royal Saint George Yacht Club clubhouse was expanded by architect John Skipton Mulvany.

The railway station, designed by John Skipton Mulvany, was completed.

1845

The Royal Saint George Yacht Club was renamed and received a royal warrant. This yacht club was formed in 1838.

1849

There was a cholera outbreak in Kingstown.

On 5 June, the Young Irlanders William Smith O'Brien, Meagher, McManus, and Donohoe were shipped on board the HMS *Swift* at Kingstown for transportation to Van Dieman's Land, the sentence of death passed at Clonmel having been commuted by the Queen.

On 5 August, the royal squadron, with ten steamers including the *Victoria and Albert* carrying the Queen, Prince Albert, the Prince of Wales, the Princess Royal, Prince Alfred, and Princess Alice anchored in Kingstown Harbour.

On 10 August, the Royal Family came by train from Westland Row and embarked at Victoria Wharf. On leaving the pier, the royal standard was lowered and raised again this was stated to be a mark of honour never before employed except for a royal personage.

The Independent Church, later Kingstown Congregational Church, on Northumberland Avenue was established.

Griffith's Valuation of Kingstown was completed.

1852

The anemometer,
a device for measuring
wind speed, was
erected on the East
Pier. It was designed by
Professor Robinson of
Trinity College Dublin.

1854

20,000 troops
embarked from
Kingstown to fight
in the Crimean War.

The Royal Saint George
Yacht Club opened.
The architect John Skipton
Mulvany designed it.

The City of Dublin Steam
Packet Company took
over the mail service.
They purchased the *Saint
Columba* and *Llewellyn*
and two other vessels.

1850

1856

1851

The population
of Kingstown
was recorded
as 10,453.

On 29 August Queen Victoria and Prince
Albert arrived from Holyhead. They landed
at Kingstown at 10.06 p.m. and spent
only a few minutes there. They arrived
at Westland Row at 10.40 p.m.

On 3 September, Queen Victoria and
Prince Albert departed from Kingstown,
following their visit to the Great
Industrial Exhibition. Their train arrived
at the station at 6.40 p.m. and they
boarded the royal yacht at 7.15 p.m.

The construction of the
Carlisle Pier commenced.

The terminal shed was completed at
the railway station. The main walls
of this shed are still in position.

The soldiers returned from the
Crimean War to Kingstown,
less many casualties.

A Russian cannon captured
in the Crimean War arrived
in Kingstown as a war trophy.
It was mounted on a metal
carriage and placed on the
Victoria Wharf, in line with
the centre of Marine Road.

The Christian Brothers'
School opened in
Eblana Avenue.

1853

1858

The HMS *Ajax* arrived in Kingstown Harbour and took up a strategic position as a guardship. It was the first of many such ships positioned in Kingstown to clearly demonstrate the might and power of Britain.

1857

There was a train accident at Kingstown station on 20 December when an engine collided with stationary carriages. Fortunately there were no injuries.

The gauge of the Dublin to Kingstown railway was altered to 5ft 3ins, and that gauge has remained to the present day. Until that time, the gauge had been 4ft 8½ins.

The Carlisle Pier was completed. This included the spur railway line with platform so that passengers could transfer directly from the train to the mail boat. The timetable was arranged so that one could arrive at the city terminus (Westland Row) thirty-five minutes before sailing time and still catch the departing boat.

New contractual arrangements were agreed between the Royal Mail and the City of Dublin Steam Packet Company for the delivery of mail to and from Holyhead. The passage time from Kingstown to Holyhead was set at three hours and forty-five minutes, with a penalty for every excess minute.

The coastguard station and cottages opened.

The congregational Church on Northumberland Avenue opened. It was demolished in the 1950s and replaced by Lee's Furniture, and later Dunnes Stores supermarket. It is now a vacant building.

1859

1860

Saint John's church opened in Mounttown.

The harbour was fully completed. The accumulated cost of construction of the harbour was estimated at £1 million.

Crosthwaite Park was developed.

St Joseph's Orphanage opened on Tivoli Road. It had relocated from St Vincent's Orphan House, Sussex Street.

1861

There was another cholera outbreak in Kingstown, resulting in 124 deaths.

The foundation stone was laid for the Presbyterian church, on York Road.

Proposals for steam ferries between Kingstown and Custom House Quay were put forward.

In February, the *Neptune* and *Industry* sank off the East Pier. Captain Boyd and others were awarded medals for bravery while attempting to rescue the seamen.

The Boyd Monument, an obelisk, was erected on the East Pier.

On 22 August, Queen Victoria and Prince Albert arrived in Kingstown. On 24 August, they went on to the Curragh where the Prince of Wales, who later became King Edward VII, had been performing military duties for some months. Then they travelled on to Killarney for a few days.

On 30 August, Queen Victoria and Prince Albert departed from Kingstown. Prince Albert died four months later.

Eglinton Park was completed.

St Joseph's Orphanage, Tivoli Road, opened.

The lifeboat house, at the start of the East Pier, was completed.

1864

Roger Casement was born at Doyle's Cottage, Lawson Terrace, in Sandycove.

HMS *Royal George* arrived in Kingstown Harbour and took up a strategic position as a guardship, replacing the HMS *Ajax*.

1863

An orphanage, now known locally as the Bird's Nest, opened in York Road. It housed homeless children.

The railway siding to the Trader's Wharf was constructed.

Dublin Builder reports that Kingstown Harbour cost £1 million to that date.

Deansgrange Cemetery opened.

The Forty Foot bathing place opened.

The lighthouse keeper's house was constructed on the West Pier.

1865

The foundation was laid for the spire tower of Mariners' church.

In October, the Royal Marine Hotel opened.

The Salthill Hotel re-opened after extensive refurbishment.

On 5 July, the USS *Sacramento*, a US warship, came to Kingstown and stayed for two weeks. It was involved in chasing a confederate ship that had not surrendered at the end of the American civil war.

1862

On 4 July, a paddle-steamer service from the Custom House to Kingstown launched. The paddle steamer, called the *Kingstown*, was 46m (150 foot) long and 12m (40 foot) wide and the journey time was about thirty minutes. The route was also served by another paddle steamer, the *Dublin*.

A proposal to erect a monument to Prince Albert at Kingstown was put forward. An unnamed resident offered to pay £200-£500 for the project.

On 29 August, the USS *Tuscarora* came in to Kingstown for supplies and repairs. While there, she was under observation from HMS *Shannon* (1855) and HMS *Ajax* (1809). Three days earlier she had docked at Queenstown, now known as Cobh, but was ordered to leave despite a gale. In Kingstown, Captain Craven and his crew were well received and attended a service at the Mariners' church. A request from the Catholic Church to allow Catholic crewmen to attend mass was refused. A banquet was arranged for the captain and crew, but the ship departed suddenly before the banquet could take place. This was the early part of the American civil war and the USS *Tuscarora* was on a mission to find ships flying the confederate flag. American warships were not welcome in British ports at the time.

There was another cholera outbreak in Kingstown and Monkstown.

The Haliday report on the sanitation and the living conditions of the poor in Kingstown was prepared. It was published in the following year.

Charles Haliday, the historian and campaigner on behalf of the poor, died.

1866

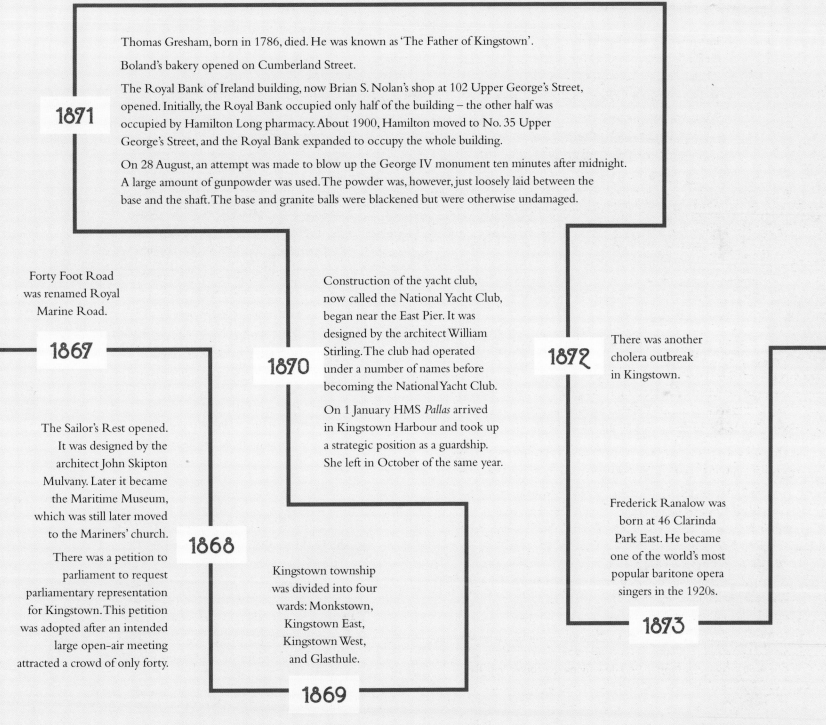

1871

Thomas Gresham, born in 1786, died. He was known as 'The Father of Kingstown'.

Boland's bakery opened on Cumberland Street.

The Royal Bank of Ireland building, now Brian S. Nolan's shop at 102 Upper George's Street, opened. Initially, the Royal Bank occupied only half of the building – the other half was occupied by Hamilton Long pharmacy. About 1900, Hamilton moved to No. 35 Upper George's Street, and the Royal Bank expanded to occupy the whole building.

On 28 August, an attempt was made to blow up the George IV monument ten minutes after midnight. A large amount of gunpowder was used. The powder was, however, just loosely laid between the base and the shaft. The base and granite balls were blackened but were otherwise undamaged.

Forty Foot Road was renamed Royal Marine Road.

1867

1870

Construction of the yacht club, now called the National Yacht Club, began near the East Pier. It was designed by the architect William Stirling. The club had operated under a number of names before becoming the National Yacht Club.

On 1 January HMS *Pallas* arrived in Kingstown Harbour and took up a strategic position as a guardship. She left in October of the same year.

1872

There was another cholera outbreak in Kingstown.

The Sailor's Rest opened. It was designed by the architect John Skipton Mulvany. Later it became the Maritime Museum, which was still later moved to the Mariners' church.

There was a petition to parliament to request parliamentary representation for Kingstown. This petition was adopted after an intended large open-air meeting attracted a crowd of only forty.

1868

Frederick Ranalow was born at 46 Clarinda Park East. He became one of the world's most popular baritone opera singers in the 1920s.

1873

Kingstown township was divided into four wards: Monkstown, Kingstown East, Kingstown West, and Glasthule.

1869

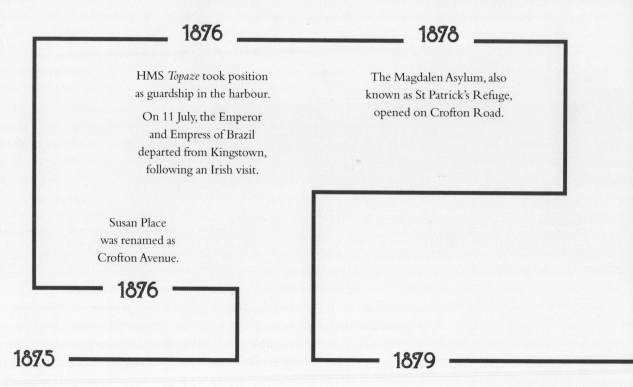

1876

HMS *Topaze* took position
as guardship in the harbour.

On 11 July, the Emperor
and Empress of Brazil
departed from Kingstown,
following an Irish visit.

1878

The Magdalen Asylum, also
known as St Patrick's Refuge,
opened on Crofton Road.

Bridget Mary Lynch was born in
Booterstown. Later she became
Sister Mary Concepta Lynch
and decorated the Dominican
Oratory on Library Road.

Michael Mallin was born.
He was commander of the
Citizen Army at Saint Stephen's
Green on Easter 1916. In 1966,
the railway station was
renamed as Mallin station.

Susan Place
was renamed as
Crofton Avenue.

1876

1874   **1875**

1879

St Michael's Hospital opened.
It was designed by the architect
John Loftus Robinson.

The HMS *Vanguard* was
accidentally struck and sunk
by the HMS *Iron Duke* at Bray
Head after leaving Kingstown.

HMS *Iron Duke* took position
as guardship in the harbour.

Charles Vignoles died. He was an
engineer and had worked with
William Dargan on the construction
of the Dublin to Kingstown railway.

The Kingstown to Dalkey tramline opened, served by horse-drawn trams.
The trams had a narrow gauge that was different from those in
the rest of the Dublin area. In particular, it was different from
that of the Dublin-Kingstown trams, and so passengers from
Dublin to Dalkey had to change trams at Marine Road.

Kingstown post office opened on Royal Marine Road.

Edward McCabe, the parish priest of Kingstown, became Archbishop of Dublin.

The Cottage Home for Little Children was founded.
Soon afterwards it moved to premises on Tivoli Road.

The Exham Commission on Local Government
examined the administration of Kingstown.

Daniel Reddin, a Fenian, died in Kingstown. Reddin had earlier suffered
five years of penal servitude for his part in the escape of two prisoners from
a prison van in Manchester in 1867. This was the incident for which the
Manchester Martyrs were hanged. By the time he was released, his health
had deteriorated to the point that he was described as a paralytic cripple.

1883

On 30 October, a loan of £16,000 was sanctioned by the Local Government Board for sewage works at the West Pier.

1882

James Joyce, writer, was born. Though he was not born in Kingstown, he had various addresses in the area, such as 23 Carysfort Avenue, Blackrock, and Martello tower, Sandycove.

1884

The HMS *Belleisle* took position as guardship in the harbour.

John Crosthwaite died. Among many developments, he was responsible for the original Royal Victoria Baths at Queen's Road. These baths were demolished in the early years of the twentieth century and were replaced by a different arrangement of baths nearby. He had been chairman of Kingstown Town Commissioners on many occasions.

1885

A steam paddle ship, the *Ireland*, was launched by the City of Dublin Steam Packet Company for use on the Kingstown to Holyhead route.

On 15 July, Kingstown Town Hall opened.

There was a serious fire at the Quaker Friends' Meeting Hall in Monkstown.

1880

1887

Howard Grubb was knighted by Queen Victoria for his inventions of optical instruments.

The Water Wags sailing club was formed.

The *Irish American Weekly* reported that 'At a meeting of the Kingstown Township Board on 1 March, Mr J.L. Robinson brought forward a motion to change the name of the township of Kingstown to Old Dunleary. After some discussion the motion was withdrawn by the proposer, until a Board more conversant with National principles was in office'. By coincidence Seán Ó hUadhaigh was born in this year. In 1922, he initiated the process that led to the naming of Dún Laoghaire. Shortly afterwards, on 17 July 1922, he wrote to *The Irish Times* and referred to the word Dunleary as 'the half-hearted effort of some planter to vocalise the old name'.

Dr Richard Robert Madden died. He was a historian, medical practitioner, and campaigner for civil rights. He had a surgery in the area of Ballygihan Avenue and practiced around Glasthule.

1881

Padraic Colum, playwright and poet, was born. Though he was not born in Kingstown, he spent much of his young life at Perrin's Row, in Sandycove.

1886

1890

The People's Park, designed by John Loftus Robinson, was opened. The park layout was changed in 1937.

The courthouse, designed by William Kaye-Perry, opened on Upper George's Street. It was demolished during the 1970s and replaced by the post office.

Joshua Pim (1869–1942), a native of Crosthwaite Park, won his first Wimbledon doubles final.

1889

John Loftus Robinson, architect, became chairman of Kingstown Town Council.

Richard Pigott died at 11 Sandycove Avenue West. He was a forger of infamous letters about Charles Stewart Parnell.

1891

The HMS *Curlew* took position as guardship in the harbour.

The Christian Institute was completed on Upper George's Street. It was designed by William Kaye-Perry and opened for business in the following year.

1888

William Kaye-Parry proposed the construction of floating swimming baths in Kingstown Harbour.

1892

The HMS *Melampus* took position as guardship in the harbour.

The tower on St Michael's church was demolished and replaced by a spire designed by John Loftus Robinson.

1895

St Joseph's Young Priests Society was established by Olivia Taaffe (1838–1918) at number 7 Eblana Terrace.

On 24 December, fifteen members of the Kingstown lifeboat crew were lost during an attempted rescue of the crew of the *Palme*. The crew of the *Palme* were rescued by another ship, the *Tearaght*.

1893

In January, the Workmen's Club opened in a converted tenement building. It was founded by Professor (Sir) William F. Barrett. Later, it moved to Lower George's Street.

Joshua Pim won his first Wimbledon singles final, and his second doubles final.

1894

Joshua Pim won his second Wimbledon singles final.

Kingstown Grammar School was founded by Revd Matthew Edward Devlin in York Road.

1898

1897

On 9 February, the steamer *Ulster* performed her trial trip from Holyhead to Kingstown in two hours and twenty-six minutes.

The electric lights in the Royal Marine Hotel were powered by their own generator.

From about this date, most premises having frontage on George's Street were obliged by the terms of their leases to rebuild their frontage in red brick.

Ireland's first petrol-driven car was imported by Dr J.F. Colohan of 26 Rock Road, in Blackrock.

From 20 to 22 July, the first live transmission of a sporting event in the world took place. Guglielmo Marconi broadcast the results of the Kingstown regatta from a steam tug to the shore, to be telephoned through to the *Daily Express* newspaper.

1899

The National Telephone Company was established in Kingstown. This event marked the arrival of the first telephones in the town.

Kingstown Urban District Council was established to replace the Kingstown Town Commissioners.

The fire station in George's Place was opened.

The National Bank building moved from Royal Marine Road to a new building at 101 Upper George's Street. This building now houses the Bank of Ireland.

1896

Leonard Alfred George Strong, writer, was born. Though not born in Kingstown, he spent much of his young life at Newtownsmith.

The tramlines to and from Dublin and to and from Dalkey were electrified. The gauge of the Kingstown to Dalkey section was also changed to match the rest of the network.

1900

The population of Kingstown Urban District was recorded as 17,356.

On 4 April, Queen Victoria arrived in Kingstown.

On 26 April, Queen Victoria departed from Kingstown.

On 30 September, Captain the Honourable Francis George Crofton, Royal Navy, long-time harbourmaster of Kingstown, died.

1903

The Kingstown Improvement Scheme 1902 was approved by parliament. This scheme led to the construction of Barrett Street, Cumberland Street, Cross Avenue, Wolfe Tone Avenue Mills Street, and Desmond Avenue.

On 21 July, King Edward VII and Queen Alexandra arrived at Kingstown. They drove to the Vice-Regal Lodge amid great enthusiasm.

The new Methodist church on Northumberland Avenue was opened.

On 26 August, Thomas Brown was knighted. He was a tobacconist at the junction of Lower George's Street and Sussex Street. He died less than a fortnight later. He had fallen ill on the previous day while collecting funds for the Dominican Convent at St Michael's Church.

The Pavilion opened in Kingstown. A leisure and entertainment complex, it included a concert hall, a roof-top garden, several smoking rooms, reading rooms, tea rooms, as well as tennis courts, mini-golf, and so on. It was later converted to a cinema after two serious fires.

1902

On 16 May, a German squadron of eight battleships, under the command of Prince Henry of Prussia, arrived in Dublin Bay, and anchored off the East Pier, Kingstown, until 22 May.

1901

The Harbour Road was renamed to Queen's Road.

Major works to reconfigure the town centre were undertaken. They continued for several years and included:

Widening of streets – The frontages of Nos 2–10 Upper George's Street were demolished and rebuilt 4.2m (14ft) back from the road.

Creation of Convent Road – Two shops, Nos 65 and 66 Lower George's Street were demolished to permit the joining of Paradise Row through to Lower George's Street.

Demolition of No. 76 Lower George's Street. No. 76 was Moynihan's wholesale grocers. It stood on the corner of Marine Road. It was demolished to create a somewhat more open vista in the town centre. Later, about 1935, McDonald's hardware at No. 76 Lower George's Street was also demolished to create the open space now on the corner.

Rebuild of Findlater's and McCullagh's – Findlater's rebuilt and expanded from No. 85 to new premises built at Nos 84 and 85. McCullagh's moved from No. 85 into new premises at Nos 82 and 83. All of these premises are included in Penney's store today.

1904

On 26 April, their Majesties King Edward VII and Queen Alexandra arrived at Kingstown. Having received addresses from the principal public bodies in Ireland, they proceeded by rail to Naas and attended the Punchestown races.

On 28 April, Their Majesties drove to Leinster Lawn, where the King laid the foundation stone of the new College of Science.

From 30 April to 3 May, Their Majesties visited Kilkenny, Waterford, and Lismore. On 3 May, they travelled from Lismore to Kingstown, where they embarked for Holyhead.

16 June became known as Bloomsday. This is the day depicted in Joyce's fictional epic, *Ulysses*, and includes events in the Kingstown and Sandycove area.

Desmond Avenue was built.

Mill's Street was built.

Wolfe Tone Avenue was built.

1906

On 31 August, a ball was held for officers of the Atlantic Fleet. A bridge was constructed from the town hall to the Pavilion for the occasion.

Dunleary Road, along the side of the railway line from Old Dunleary to Crofton Road, opened.

The Grand Central Hotel was opened by Philip Hynes on Marine Road. This may be the hotel over Philip Hynes pub at 1 Upper George's Street, which faced on to Marine Road.

1905

Edward Lee and Company opened on Upper George's Street. The shop is now Dunnes Stores. The upper floors were originally intended as staff quarters, but were later converted to a hotel (The Avenue Hotel).

Barrett Street and Dominick Street were built.

On 10 July, the King and Queen, with Princess Victoria, arrived at Kingstown, and drove to the Irish International Exhibition. They returned to Britain from Kingstown two days later.

The Municipal Technical School opened on Eblana Avenue.

1908

From 24 to 27 August, five battleships of the Atlantic Fleet, under the command of Vice-Admiral Sir Assheton G. Curzon-Howe, docked at Kingstown.

1907

From 8 to 12 November, four battleships of the Atlantic Fleet, under the command of HSH Prince Louis of Battenberg, docked at Kingstown.

May's Shop, on the corner of Patrick Street and Lower George's Street, opened. It closed in 1981 and is now the O2 mobile phone shop.

The Dún Laoghaire Golf Club, founded as Kingstown Golf Club, opened.

The Dún Laoghaire Club, on Eblana Avenue, was founded.

Dungar Terrace was built at the back of the shop of Edward Lee & Co Ltd. It was intended to house the shop employees.

York Street was renamed as York Road.

1909

1910

Kingstown in Pictures –  Visible Kingstown

Streets and Shopping in Kingstown

The layout of most of the streets of Dunleary was planned around 1816 or 1817. This was a time when much of the area was open, unfenced land. The backbone of the town was formed by a straight, long, main street, later named George's Street, and still later divided into Upper and Lower George's Streets. Most of the other streets were placed at right angles to it. This street quickly became a trading street, with many shops and trades offering a wide range of goods and services. Gradually, the trades moved away and it became mainly a street of retailers and services, including banks and insurance.

Thom's Directory reports that the street was 'Macadamized' as early as 1850. This form of surfacing, also known as Macadamisation, was not like the modern form of tarmac. Macadamisation meant that the street was constructed of layers of broken stone of predetermined size, properly laid and cambered.

Upper George's Street, Looking West Towards Dublin

This photo, published in 1877, but probably taken up to ten years earlier, is the earliest-known photo of the main street of the town. It seems reasonably clear of animal droppings, despite the number of horse-drawn vehicles that would have been around at that time. The tramlines for the Dalkey horse tram had not yet been laid. The first horse tram would run in 1879.

The location is Upper George's Street at Mulgrave Street junction. The camera is looking in the direction of Dublin.

UPPER GEORGE'S STREET LOOKING EAST, TOWARDS SANDYCOVE/GLASTHULE 1898

This picture shows the same streetscape, seen from the opposite direction, some years later. It is dated from about 1898 and was taken from the upper deck of the No. 7 tram. It is likely that the tram driver cooperated by stopping the tram at the appropriate time and location.

The picture shows Upper George's Street at the junction with Marine Road, then Royal Marine Road, on the left, and with Patrick Street on the right.

By 1898, the street had been cobbled. The era of horse trams had come and gone and electric trams had been operating for two years.

In the centre of the picture, P. Redmond and Company, wine merchants, occupied one of the most visible sites in the town. It is very interesting to note how they created a monogram using the intertwined initials of the company (R and Co): this was displayed very prominently between the main shop windows. Redmonds was a very fine building with an elaborate exterior featuring canopied windows and ornamentation at the roof level. The shop front itself is an excellent example of the best design and craftsmanship of the period.

Redmond's pub, later Cunnion's, was demolished about 1912 when the Ulster Bank came to town. The Ulster Bank has held that prime site to the present day, despite a number of rebuilds.

Just visible to the extreme left of the picture, beside the small girl, is the corner of a building with a piece of cornice which is typical of a Victorian shop front. There were, indeed, shops right up to the junction, in the area which is now unbuilt in front of St Michael's church. That shop on the corner was Moynihans, a wholesale grocer and spirit merchant. It was also demolished as part of the road-widening initiative and was not rebuilt. Moynihans did eventually re-open in a different location.

Visible in the centre of the street are the special arrangements for trams to meet. A better example of these arrangements can be seen in Lower George's Street (page 42). Further down the street on the right, we can see trees. Lee's shop, now Dunnes Stores, on the junction with Northumberland Road, had not yet been built. That section of the street was occupied by houses with long gardens to the front where large trees grew. Just visible in the mist is the tall building of the Royal Bank of Ireland. This is the premises now occupied by Brian S. Nolan, draper. The bank building had a plainer frontage then.

Very few of the frontages shown in this picture have been preserved.

DEMOLITION AND STREET WIDENING, 1900

By 1900, the town was getting a new look. The original leases of the town were running out and the landlords were putting pressure on shop-owners to improve their facades, and many of them had done so. However, the town centre was rather cramped. It was considered too tightly packed for a main street of a town with aspirations of grandeur. The original 1817 layout of the street was just sufficiently wide for two horse carriages to meet, and to have a footpath on either side. The planners may have wished to create a town square in the centre of the town, but this would have been too costly. Instead, they opted for some lesser initiatives.

1 The shop frontages of Nos 2–10 on Upper George's Street were demolished. This is the block which faces you as you come up Marine Road. In 2015 terms, this is the block from Facet Jewellers to the vacant premises which was most recently occupied by Danske Bank, formerly National Irish Bank.

2 Moynihans Wholesale Grocery, which occupied the corner of Marine Road in front of the church, was also demolished.

3 Numbers 65, 66, and 66a on Lower George's Street were demolished to create an opening from Lower George's Street into Paradise Row, which was then renamed Convent Road. These shops were, respectively, The Dublin Meat Company, Singer Sewing Machine Company, and Miss Sheridan, victualler.

The photograph opposite, taken while the demolition was in progress, shows Upper George's Street at the junction with Patrick Street. On the extreme left, we can see that No. 4 has been demolished. Number 4, which had been the bakery of Herron Connolly and Company, was a very ornate building that proudly proclaimed in stone that it was 'Bakers to the Queen'. Numbers 5–10 were also highly ornamented. Number 3, the premises of Charles Cook, always appeared rather out-of-place among those good-quality buildings. Similarly, Waters shop seems positively temporary. Charles Cook, photographer and bazaar-owner, had only been in No. 3 for a short number of years. His sign shows 'Rebuilding – must clear', an effort to tempt shoppers in the direction of his bargain wares. He re-opened after the rebuild and continued in business for many years. William Waters, watchmaker, did not re-open. His place was taken by the White Heather Laundry after the rebuild.

The photograph was clearly a time exposure and the people are posed and have been asked to stand still. Some conformed well, others not so well, but clearly one or more people walked right across the field of vision and left ghostly tracks on the negative. The man in the door of the bar stayed perfectly still.

Although the picture is uncredited, the photographer was probably Charles Cook, wishing to remember his last day trading on that site.

The outcome of the demolition and subsequent rebuild was:

1   Number 1, Hynes' pub was not demolished. It did not need to be, since it was already set back from the building line. It was rebuilt as the Provincial Bank of Ireland some years later. It is now Facet Jewellers.

2   Numbers 2–9 got new frontages, which were built very rapidly and are red brick with little or no ornamentation. These can be seen on the upper floors of Nos 2–9 today.

3   Number 10 was not immediately rebuilt and was a vacant site for 10 years or more. It was then rebuilt as the Kingstown Picture House. It had many changes of use and appearance before being finally rebuilt as the National Irish Bank, with a facade similar to Nos 2–9.

TOWN CENTRE AFTER THE STREET WIDENING, c. 1905

This postcard (left) was photographed from the upper window of McKeon's shop, now Permanent TSB Bank, on the corner of Mulgrave Street and Upper George's Street.

The street was probably at the peak of its attractiveness at that time. Many of the shops had been forced to rebuild frontages in red brick as the original ninety-nine-year leases of the Longford and de Vesci estates became due for renewal, and those landlords insisted that the tenants should conform to their concept of an attractive town.

The awnings on many of the shops were an attractive feature; but they were also a necessity. The dyes used in Victorian materials were prone to fading and a dress left in a south-facing, unprotected window for several days would be likely to fade.

UPPER GEORGE'S STREET, c. 1900

This is the junction with Upper Glenageary Road on the left and Longford Terrace on the right. The name of Longford Terrace was subsequently changed to Park Road to avoid confusion with Longford Terrace in Monkstown.

Although this part of George's Street had some very fine buildings, it did not seem to match the popularity of the other end of the street. Much of this section of the town has been preserved, particularly at the level of the upper floors.

UPPER GEORGE'S STREET, c. 1907

The National Bank, at 101 Upper George's Street, in the centre of this picture, moved there in 1900 from its previous position in Royal Marine Road. The National Bank was taken over by the Bank of Ireland in 1966 or many years thereafter; it had two branches in the town, almost facing each other. Some years ago, the branch at Anglesea Buildings opposite was closed.

At 102 Upper George's Street was the Royal Bank, sharing its premises with Hamilton Long Chemists. Later the chemist moved across the road and the bank expanded. The Royal Bank became part of AIB about 1966. Later, AIB developed new premises further up the street, and the old bank became the curtain shop of Brian S. Nolan.

The building on the right was the courthouse. An earlier courthouse was located in the town hall, and a sign over a side door of the town hall still indicates 'Courthouse'. The relocation of the courthouse to this site made it much more convenient for the Dublin Metropolitan Police, whose barracks were located just behind it.

On the left of the picture is the shop of Edward Lee & Co., which was a new addition at the time of the photo. The Avenue Hotel, also owned by Lees, occupied the upper floors and operated a strict temperance policy. Prior to the construction of Lees, the site had houses set back from the road with long gardens and trees.

LOWER GEORGE'S STREET FROM THE NO. 7 TRAM, LOOKING WEST TOWARDS DUBLIN, 1898

The photo below was taken at the junction of Lower George's Street and Sussex Street. All of the frontages on the left side were rebuilt in the following few years. The first two shops on the right, Nos 86 and 87, have retained traditional facades and plain upper halves. No. 86 traded as a tobacconist for many years under the name Sir Thomas Brown. The third premises, No. 88, which was under construction at the time, has traded as a pub under various names in the recent past and is now known as Whiskey Fare.

When the tramlines were laid for electric trams in 1898, the shopkeepers insisted that the lines to and from the city would not be laid side-by-side.

Having two lines would inhibit the loading and unloading of deliveries and more importantly would prevent shoppers from driving their carriages right up to the shop door. The compromise was that the lines would overlap along most of the street, but would separate at tram stops as shown in this picture.

Most of the frontages on the left side were altered in the decade following this picture. These frontages, dating from the early 1900s, have been preserved at the level of the upper floors.

LOWER GEORGE'S STREET, c. 1903

Starting from the left, the doorway is that of Rings, building contractors, and the sign reads 'Drainage Works'. The present building on that site shows the initials of John Ring & Co., 1904. The section shown is now occupied by the offices of Richard Boyd Barrett, TD.

Watsons and Hands shops moved from there about 1907. Watsons was replaced by Tyler's Shoes, and No. 90 has been associated with shoes for much of its life since.

The building with a triple-gable frontage was Penrose Morrisons department store at the time of the photo. Later it changed its name to George B. Morrison. In 1926 the shop was occupied by Woolworths, and later by a carpet showrooms. The most recent occupant was Marks and Spencer, but the building is unoccupied in 2015.

Further up the street is Findlaters. Findlaters had been rebuilt and doubled in size just a couple of years earlier. Findlaters had a chain of grocery shops throughout Dublin and each of them had a prominent clock. At the time of the rebuild, it happened that Convent Road was being created opposite Findlaters, and so a third face was added to the clock to make it visible from the new road. The previous clock had two faces. The Findlater shop now forms half of Penneys.

CUMBERLAND STREET FROM THE NO. 7 TRAM, LOOKING TOWARDS DUBLIN, 1898

Many of the houses on Cumberland Street were already 100 years old when this picture was taken just before 1900. The camera was positioned on the back of the upper deck of the Dalkey-bound No. 7 tram, and pointed towards Dublin as the tram moved through the York Street junction into Lower George's Street. Clearly, the tram driver cooperated by stopping the tram, and a coal wagon passed behind it, from Clarence Street through to York Road.

The tramlines had just been electrified in 1896 with overhead cabling, and the new poles had an ornamental base. Many of these tram-poles have remained in place through to today, including the pole on the left, now mounted with street lighting. It is perhaps surprising to us nowadays that electric trams pre-dated electric street lighting, and so the only street lighting in this picture is provided by two gaslights. These lights were very low by modern standards of street lighting, but there were good reasons. Firstly, the gaslights needed a lot of maintenance and secondly, the light output was very low, and insufficient for mounting high up a pole. Indeed, street lighting in those days did not attempt to light the full street. It was mainly intended to provide points of light to guide travellers home.

The first buildings on the left were those of the White family, who had a small coal merchant business and a smithy. These and all of the other buildings on the left side were demolished about 1904 and were replaced by a redbrick municipal housing scheme that still stands there today, despite internal modifications.

The first shop on the right was, in more recent years, the Cumberland Inn, but is vacant at the time of writing.

In the distant mist beyond the end of the street, a large building looms. This is the Salthill Hotel.

JAUNTING CAR ROYAL MARINE ROAD

Images of Kingstown were widely traded in the USA and produced for sale to Irish emigrants by various publishers. An image showing a jaunting car and the local church would have been ideally suited to that market.

The picture shows Royal Marine Road, later renamed as Marine Road. The jaunting car, which was long associated with Killarney, is also seen in many pictures in the area of the piers and the railway station in Kingstown.

Visible in the background is St Michael's church, with the old church tower and clock. The tower was located directly behind the main altar. It was replaced by a much taller spire designed by John Loftus Robinson in 1894 and built shortly thereafter. The new spire was located much closer to the corner of the church site. In 1965, the church suffered a disastrous fire and was demolished. The spire remains.

The present-day numbering of the houses on Marine Road starts with No. 2 on the corner of Eblana Avenue. There is no No. 1. This picture shows that No. 1 was in the grounds of St Michael's church. It was shown in the 1893 directories with Mrs Ennis as the occupant, but had been demolished before the maps of the new century were surveyed. It is likely that the demolition was required for the rebuild of the church spire.

THE HARBOUR AND SURROUNDING AREA

Since the development of the camera, the East Pier has been a mecca for photographers. It has been a place for leisure, for strolling, for people-watching, and for listening to music at the bandstand.

Construction of the pier commenced in 1817 and moved very rapidly. As the pier was extended, iron rails were placed on it to facilitate the horse-drawn carts, which carried the stone. These rails were part of a network of rails known as 'the Metals', which stretched right back to Dalkey Quarry and other quarries.

The pier is about 1.3km (0.8 miles) in length. It has two levels suitable for walking and a wall about 1.5m (5ft) high on the seaward side of the upper level. The walls slope gradually on the seaward side. They are close to vertical on the harbour side, but not enough to facilitate ships coming alongside. A modern platform has, therefore, been placed on a section of the pier to allow boats and ships coming alongside at that section. A lighthouse and a defensive battery with associated buildings were constructed at the end of the pier.

The West Pier is an equally powerful structure, but overshadowed in terms of popularity by its slightly elder sister.

The George IV monument once stood proud on Queen's Road. It still does, but can easily go unnoticed amongst the surrounding trees, or against the backdrop of the Lexicon Library.

The Town Hall, now the County Hall, railway station, and three yacht clubs all show Victorian craftsmanship in stone.

KINGSTOWN FROM THE EAST PIER, c. 1863

The oldest known view of the town from the East Pier can be dated to about 1863. At the time it was taken, by H.D. Brown from London, everything in this picture was quite new. Brown also had an address at 75 Lower George's Street. His premises is now occupied by the Educational Building Society. The fact that there are no people and no shadows suggest that it may have been taken early on a cloudy morning, at low tide.

A small piece of the upper deck of the pier, which was laid with flagstones, can be seen in the bottom left corner. The lower deck at this time was likely to have been a gravel surface, but shows no trace of wheel ruts or animal droppings. The ornamental pillars and chains are a clear indication that this section of the pier was never intended for ships or boats to moor alongside.

The small building just above water level in the left of picture is the lifeboat house. It was brand new, having been under construction in 1861. The arched opening in the granite building facilitated the easy launching of the boat. The building is still in perfect condition and is used by the Royal National Lifeboat Institution.

Just above the lifeboat house can be seen the cabman's shelter, a small but ornate roadside hut that provided shelter to the jarveys who plied their trade carrying passengers to and from the pier for their morning or afternoon stroll.

The road that runs across the centre of the picture, behind the harbour wall, was then called the Harbour Road. Later it was renamed as Queen's Road. At that time, the road turned inland about 200m (219 yards) from the left of this picture. It did not continue along the coast. Just out of shot on the right of the picture was the obelisk monument to King George IV.

In the centre of the picture, a three-part stairs is visible. The lower part of the stairs is from the level of the Harbour Road to the level of The Metals. For most of its journey, The Metals was on the landward side of the mainline railway, but along the stretch in this picture, it ran on the seaward side, between the mainline railway and the Harbour Road.

The middle piece of stairs is from the level of The Metals to the roof over the mainline railway. The mainline railway had opened in 1844 as the Kingstown–Dalkey atmospheric railway, powered by a vacuum created by a static engine in Dalkey. The atmospheric railway ceased in 1854, and the line was reconfigured for steam locomotives. By 1863, the Dublin, Wicklow, and Wexford railway train could take passengers as far as Wicklow or Rathdrum, but had not yet reached Enniscorthy or Wexford. The section of line across the harbour in this picture was in a 'cut and cover' tunnel at this time, and so cannot be seen directly here. However, a piece of fencing can be seen on a section of the tunnel roof. This fencing surrounds a vent in the roof to allow egress of steam and smoke. Years later, the roof was removed, and the railway continued in a cutting. However, at the time of writing, over 150 years later, this section has recently been re-roofed.

The higher level of the stairs is the entrance of the harbourmaster's office, which was a cottage-style building. Just beyond the railway, on the extreme right of the picture, is the harbourmaster's house (1845). At the date of this photo, the harbourmaster was Captain William Hutchison (1793–1881), the first and longest-serving harbourmaster.

Seven houses on Haddington Terrace (1835) can be seen in the left of the picture. To gain maximum advantage from the harbour view, these houses have a dual-level bay window. They are numbered from the right. It is interesting to note that house No. 3 did not have a bay window in this picture, but a bay window has been added at some later stage to match the other houses in the terrace.

Visible behind Haddington Terrace is the roof and transept of the Mariner's church (1837). At the time, the church was a functional building, very tall, but largely devoid of decoration. It is possible that the spire (1865), designed by William Raffles Brown, was under construction at the time of this photograph, but it cannot be seen above the roofs of the terrace.

Many other embellishments, including castellated-coping and pinnacles, were added at about the same time.

Gresham Terrace is visible on the right of the picture. The imposing Georgian building with twelve windows across its front is Hayes' Royal Hotel (built around 1828) on Gresham Terrace. The hotel was set on open ground over 200m (219 yards) inland from the harbour, which means that the hotel looks less imposing than might be expected. Directly in line between the photographer and the hotel, but not visible in this picture, was the freshwater reservoir to provide water for ships. This reservoir was lost in the construction of the Lexicon building (2014).

A church tower is visible in the centre back of the picture. This was the Kingstown Independent Church (1849) on Northumberland Avenue. Two aisles and a tower, designed by William Raffles Brown, were added in 1859/60 when it became the Congregational Church. The church was demolished and replaced by Lee's furniture shop, and later by Dunnes Stores supermarket. It is now a vacant building.

The dark building to the left of the church tower, at the centre of the photo, is the Dublin Metropolitan Police F Division Barracks.

Visible below the church tower, between the barracks and the hotel, are a number of small houses. These houses are on Stable Lane, leading from Upper George's Street to the stables of the hotel. Later, this lane was entered through an arch on Upper George's Street, now at the side of Brian S. Nolan's premises.

Construction of the Royal Marine Hotel commenced just about the time this photo was taken. For many years it would have dominated the centre of any photo taken from this area of the East Pier. Nowadays, the view is dominated by the Lexicon Library (2014).

THE LIFEBOAT HOUSE, 1860s

The first lifeboat to occupy the lifeboat house (1861) was the *Princess Royal*, and the name is shown on the door. The lifeboat service has always been financed by voluntary donations. The National Yacht Club had not been built when this photo was taken.

KINGSTOWN EAST PIER, 1904

Three postcards of the same view in the same year illustrate some of the many postcard styles of the period. These postcards are based upon black-and-white photos, tinted and touched up by hand

KINGSTOWN, c. 1903

Picturesque Co Dublin.
Kingstown Harbour.

Postcard printers also stretched the imagination and used artistic licence to a very great extent as in this postcard from the Oilette Series by Tuck & Sons of London. The view is distorted and no ship ever docked in that way.

KINGSTOWN EAST PIER FROM THE LAWRENCE COLLECTION, 1904

The photo below shows the Pavilion shortly after its opening. Apart from a redesign of the Pavilion, this view remained constant through to the 1960s.

QUEEN'S ROAD AND THE VICTORIA BATHS, 1893

Taken from the bay window upstairs at No. 4 Marine Terrace, looking out over the old Victoria Baths towards Sandycove and the Joyce Tower, this photo presents some difficulties of interpretation. A road-widening initiative, in about 1921, swept away virtually all of the buildings in the foreground and the large houses on the right, so that no trace of them remains today. After the road widening, new baths were built in the area of the white-walled house. Those baths, now disused, will be familiar to many Dún Laoghaireites.

The location is Queen's Road, at the junction with Longford Terrace East, now Park Road, and Marine Parade. The location of Teddy's ice cream, a familiar landmark, is just out of shot on the right. At that time, Marine Parade was the narrow lane visible on the right of the picture above the horses. The train passes underneath the road at this junction, and the cutting for the train beyond the junction is visible in the right of the picture.

The cottage shown is that of the caretaker of the baths. She was a Mrs Doherty. The wrought-iron arch over the gate of the cottage reads 'Royal Victoria Baths'. The entrance to the baths is by way of a ramp behind railings to the right of the cottage. The baths are 'Open Daily for Ladies and Gentlemen – Hot, Cold, and Tepid Baths'. The proprietor of the baths at the time was Mr John Chambly.

When the baths were established in 1843 by Mr John Crosthwaite, they were a very important feature to maintain a satisfactory level of hygiene in a town that had no public water system and inadequate sewerage. As time progressed, the wealthier citizens were able to install bathrooms; but the poorer people could not afford such luxuries.

In the bottom right of the picture, the tracks of 'The Metals' can be faintly seen. They were still used by the horse-drawn carts from the quarries in Dalkey. The rails crossed over the railway at this point, and ran along between Queen's Road and the railway.

QUEEN'S ROAD, THE METALS AND THE EAST PIER, 1893

This photo was taken the same day, and from the same bay window as the previous picture. The railway runs diagonally across the picture in a cutting between high walls, but the tracks cannot be seen. Beside the railway, horse-drawn carts can be seen pulling their loads of stone along The Metals, the tracks of which cannot be seen either. Another piece of The Metals track can be seen turning on to the East Pier.

Two, or possibly three, paddle steamers can be seen at the Carlisle Pier. These were the mail ships of the City of Dublin Steam Packet Company, which plied the route to Holyhead. A large masted ship can be seen further down on the Victoria Wharf. This has been identified as the troopship HMT *Himalaya*.

KINGSTOWN HARBOUR. 2899. W.L.

QUEEN'S ROAD, 1893

This picture suggests that the Victorians were proud of their architecture and did not wish to have it obscured by trees and vegetation. Apart from the cabin in the centre, all of the buildings in this picture were at least fifteen years old and seem to sit proud in the stark environment. All of the buildings are still standing in 2015 and were largely unmodified externally.

The level of the road surface seems to have been raised over the years since 1893. Furthermore, the level of the pier at this point has been raised considerably, but the original level is still shown by a narrow ramp on the left as you enter the pier from Queen's Road today.

The buildings shown, starting from the left, are:

1. The harbourmaster's office, a small single-storey building now located at the side of the Lexicon Library and awaiting refurbishment in 2015.
2. The harbourmaster's house, built for Captain Hutchinson, the first and longest-serving harbourmaster. At the date of this photograph, the harbourmaster was the Hon. Francis George Crofton, Capt. RN. The house was later named Moran House and is now in the grounds of the Lexicon Library.
3. The Town Hall, now the County Hall, designed by John Loftus Robinson in 1878 and restored on a number of occasions. It is now the seat of local government for the county of Dún Laoghaire Rathdown.
4. The railway station, designed by John Skipton Mulvany (1813–1870) and constructed in the 1840s. The ticket hall, seen in this picture, has been converted into a luxury restaurant.
5. The George IV monument, erected to commemorate the 1821 visit of George IV to Dunleary, which was then renamed Kingstown in his honour. The monument sits on a protruding part of the natural bedrock of the area.
6. Royal Irish Yacht Club, completed in 1850, to a design by John Skipton Mulvany.
7. Royal St George Yacht Club, completed in 1843, to a design also by John Skipton Mulvany with later extensions added around 1864.
8. The Kingstown Yacht Club, completed in 1870, to a design by William Sterling. Note that this yacht club had various changes of names, but is listed as Kingstown Yacht Club in *Thom's Directory* of 1893. It is now the National Yacht Club.

QUEEN'S ROAD AND THE GEORGE IV MONUMENT, c. 1893

Within months of his coronation as king, George IV visited Ireland. He landed at Howth, but departed from Dunleary, which was then renamed Kingstown in his honour. The harbour was an active construction site at the time, and its walls extended out quite a distance, particularly on the East Pier.

The obelisk was erected a couple of years later and was controversial from the start. It represented the dominance of the imperialist foreign monarchy. The obelisk, and the king himself, became the target of the stand-up comedians of the day. Chief among them was William Makepeace Thackeray, a poet who toured America lecturing on the lives of the four Georges. He described the monument as 'a hideous obelisk, stuck on four fat balls, and surmounted by a crown on a cushion'.

The monument was the subject of various attacks over the years. It was restored after being the subject of an attack by nationalist sympathisers in the 1970s, which severely damaged one of the balls.

GEORGE IV MONUMENT AND CARLISLE PIER, c. 1866

This early photo of the George IV monument shows, with remarkable clarity, from the broken stones on the road right through to the piers.

The Carlisle Pier opened in 1859 and brought the railway right to the mail boat berth. The early picture shows a basic open shelter on the pier. A guardship is visible in the background between the monument and the Carlisle Pier. This is probably HMS *Royal George*. Guard ships were kept in the harbour as a reminder of the might of the imperial power.

The pier was named after George Howard, 7th Earl of Carlisle (1804–1864), who served as Lord Lieutenant of Ireland for most of the period from 1855 until his death. By all accounts, he was well liked. After an earlier period in Ireland, he had been presented with a roll measuring over 400m (437 yards) in length, inscribed with the well wishes of hundreds of thousands of his Irish subjects. The roll is now held at Maynooth University.

QUEEN'S ROAD AND THE VICTORIA FOUNTAIN, c. 1903

By 1903, public tree planting along the road had changed the appearance of Queen's Road. Queen Victoria had visited Kingstown in 1900 and spent eight minutes on the quay before driving down Crofton Road to avoid the town centre, and heading off in the direction of Dublin city. The fountain was ordered from the Scottish firm of MacFarland but the queen did not live long enough to see it erected. As a symbol of British royalty, the fountain has been the target of attacks on numerous occasions, most notoriously on 25 March 1981 when it was demolished using a winch attached to an adjacent tree. It was repaired and restored to its original position in 2003 with help from the original Scottish foundry that cast it.

The railway, to the right of the road, was covered in this area for many years, but the cover had been removed by 1903, as had The Metals. In this picture, Queen's Road seems to be much closer to level than it appeared in earlier pictures. It appears to have been filled and raised. The overall impression is that of a much more significant road.

END OF THE CARLISLE PIER, c.1870

This picture was published in various formats including this stereoview, sold in the US. There is an artistic quality about the picture. It may be from the early work of Robert French. It shows the end of the Carlisle Pier. The boy is sitting on the edge of the circular railway turntable. In the days of steam, it was necessary to have a turntable at every rail terminus. Additionally, a second line was required so that the engine which pulled the front of the train could be turned around and sent down to the other end for the return journey. Visible in the background are the faint images of the Royal St George Yacht Club and the town.

RMS MUNSTER AND RMS LEINSTER, 1889

The City of Dublin Steam Packet Company won the contract for mail boat services from 1859 on the Kingstown–Holyhead route. It immediately commissioned four paddle steamers (with paddlewheels of 10m (34ft) in diameter), named after the four provinces of Ireland. They plied the route for more than thirty years. The contract required a speed of 17.5 knots and a maximum route time of three hours and forty-five minutes, with penalties imposed for every minute thereafter.

This picture, from August 1889, shows the RMS *Munster* berthed on the east side of the Carlisle Pier.

The RMS *Leinster* at anchor between the Carlisle Pier and the East Pier, with the outline of some of the major buildings of the town in the background.

RMS IRELAND, 1889

The photo on the right, also from August 1889, shows the 'Russian Trophy', a Crimean War cannon in the foreground, and the paddle-steamer RMS *Ireland* in the middle distance. In the background is the shed on the Carlisle Pier, with the funnels of another paddle steamer peeping over it. The camera position is behind the large shed at the railway station.

As the first generation of paddle steamers on the Kingstown–Holyhead route neared the end of their useful life, the City of Dublin Steam Packet Company began to look for replacements. The RMS *Ireland* was commissioned in 1885 and was larger than the earlier paddle steamers. However, by the time she was launched, she was already out of date, as screw-driven ships dominated the waves. She was withdrawn from service by about 1889.

THE RUSSIAN TROPHY

In the days before modern media, when Britain won a war they considered it necessary to display the spoils of war. Many Irishmen participated in the Crimean War from 1854–1856 and when the war ended, the victors displayed the captured Russian cannon throughout Britain and Ireland. The cannon, which came to Kingstown in 1857, had no mounting, and a steel carriage was ordered from the Royal Armoury at Woolwich. The cannon and its carriage, ornamental rather than functional, can be seen here. In terms of present-day Dún Laoghaire, that original cannon location is at the northern edge of the roundabout near the railway station. The cannon was still in that position when Queen Victoria visited in 1900 and can be seen in photographs of that day.

Sometime after 1900, the cannon was moved to a position on Queen's Road close to the public baths and it was mounted on a wooden carriage. In the 1940s it was taken away from public view and stored in the maintenance yard of the People's Park for many years. In 1974, the cannon was re-mounted and was placed in its present position on a pedestal on the East Pier.

The following are the basic facts of the gun:

Country of origin	Russia
Length	2,750mm
Bore	153mm
Weight	122 poods (1 pood = 16.38kg) = 1998kg
Symbol	Double-headed eagle
Serial No.	p84
Arrived in Kingstown	1857, following Treaty of Paris 1856
Date of manufacture	1799

This gun is one of the oldest public artefacts in Dún Laoghaire.

QUEEN VICTORIA'S VISIT, 1861

Queen Victoria came to Kingstown on 22 April 1861 at the start of her visit to Ireland with her husband, Prince Albert, and three of their nine children, Alfred, Helena and Alice. It was not her first visit to the town, nor would it be her last. She had departed through Kingstown on her 1849 visit, and had also been in the town in 1853.

On this occasion, the royal yacht *Victoria and Albert* docked at the Carlisle Pier late in the evening, and the royal party slept on board. In the morning, the lord lieutenant visited. The Carlisle Pier was filled with enthusiastic crowds. This is the only known photo of the event. The mast of the royal yacht with a flag aloft can just be discerned in the background.

Although the visit was private, Mr R. Chambers, chairman of the Kingstown Town Commissioners, requested that he should be allowed to present a formal address of welcome and the request was granted. Quickly, the royal party boarded the train and were off.

The Queen spent eight days in Ireland, paying a visit to her son Edward (later Edward VII) who was stationed at the Curragh. She returned via Kingstown on 29 August, to the sound of a twenty-one-gun salute from HMS *Ajax*, the guardship stationed in the harbour.

VICTORIA WHARF AND THE HARBOUR, c.1866

This photo was taken from the upper floors of one of the houses of Gresham Terrace, which is now the location of the car park of the Dún Laoghaire Shopping Centre. Neither the town hall nor the Pavilion had been built.

From the left, the buildings shown are:

The railway station designed by John Skipton Mulvany

The sailors coffee house

The Harbour Constable's Office (this is the small granite building with a porch and is often confused with a later building, the Sailors Rest)

The hexagonal building may have been a ticket office

The office of the City of Dublin Steam Packet Company (with signage). This office was demolished about this time and is not shown on the 1866 map

VICTORIA WHARF MAP AND MARKETS, c. 1866

The Victoria Wharf was constructed in 1837 and was named in honour of the newly crowned queen. Until the Carlisle Pier was completed in 1859, the Victoria Wharf was the terminus for mail steamers operated by the City of Dublin Steam Packet Company and was used by visiting ships, including those associated with various royal visits.

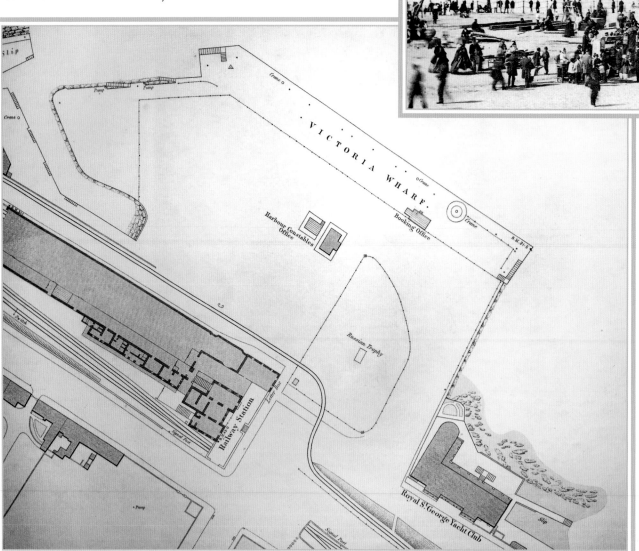

Today the wharf has largely disappeared under the car ferry terminal.

After 1859, when the mail boats moved away from this wharf, it was used for markets, especially on the days of local regattas. The pictures appear to show a wide range of activities on the wharf, with people in the background watching the boats while those in the foreground are selling what appear to be foodstuffs.

VICTORIA WHARF AND THE HARBOUR, c. 1898

A beautiful but sad view. It will inspire different emotions in different people. Much of the Victoria Wharf has been grassed and fenced off, indicating that the wharf is little used for commercial shipping. The cranes, which were quite small, are inactive and the shed is empty. The nearby Carlisle Pier is where all of the action takes place. The Crimean War cannon is still prominently displayed on the wharf.

The last opportunity to see this central area of the town as a wide, open vista was about this time. A few years later, in 1903, the Pavilion was built and it gradually encroached across the park area. Today, little of this view can be seen.

VICTORIA FOUNTAIN AND DAVY STEPHENS

Davy Stephens was probably the best-known newspaperman in the country. His pitch, which he defended stoutly, was around the fountain and the town hall. He also had a paper shop at 27 Upper George's Street. The shop is now vacant. Notoriously, it was the premises of the Swastika Laundry for many years.

He was the individual who met you as you entered the country and who said goodbye when you left. He courted the cameras and was regularly photographed with the rich and famous.

TRADERS WHARF, c.1893

The Traders Wharf was constructed in the 1870s to provide better facilities for loading and unloading coal and general cargo. The smaller coal harbour behind it was shallow and prone to silting. A twin-track railway ran for much of the length of the wharf, and a turntable was installed at the end of the wharf to turn the train engine. The picture shows the crane operated by Irish Lights, which was used to load buoys and other maritime navigation artefacts on to the Irish Lights ships for delivery or for placement to mark the position of sea hazards. Buoys, ready for positioning, can be seen in the right of the picture. Chains for anchoring the buoys can be seen under the crane. Visible at the foot of the derrick crane is the barrel of a cannon. It is not known what purpose it might have served there.

The ship in the background, with flags flying, is the HMT *Himalaya*, a naval troop ship.

MAN ON BOAT-PIER, c. 1893

There is a tiny cove and boathouse on the Traders Wharf, and this tiny pier is the edge of the cove. The crane seen in the Traders Wharf picture is visible in the top right. The names on the buoys awaiting installation can easily be seen: Blackwater, Splaugh, and Kish. All of these buoys were marked by Irish Lights.

The man with the bowler hat, on the pier, is probably not just an innocent bystander. It is a posed picture, and this man, or a man like him appears in many of the Lawrence pictures. Again, HMT *Himalaya* is visible.

ENTERTAINMENT AND LEISURE IN KINGSTOWN

A quick examination of the census records of Longford Terrace, Monkstown for 1901 shows that more than 50 per cent of the residents declared annuities, rents, and dividends as their source of income. In such an environment, there was much time for entertainment and leisure activities.

The annual regattas in the town were among the highlights of the social calendar and were normally held in July. In addition to the yacht racing in the harbour, there were land-based events including fireworks displays, balls, and concerts.

Before the construction of the Town Hall, the Kingstown Concert Rooms in Sussex Place was the main venue for local entertainment. The events there ranged from exotic international performers to local amateur clubs. It also provided a range of lectures, mainly on scientific topics. Another venue was the Assembly Rooms in Corrig Avenue, where Thomas Dockrell was the proprietor.

There are records of major public concerts on the lawn of the Royal Marine. The programme for the evening of 29 July 1875 shows a concert in costume with a full range of artists singing selections from *Il Trovatore, Maritana, Bohemian Girl,* and *Madame Angot.* They were supported by a band and chorus of fifty. This concert had Chinese lanterns, balloon ascents, illuminations, fireworks, and a grand discharge of shells and rockets.

Sporting activities were important. Cricket was played in Monkstown on the pitch at Hollyville Park, which is now Richmond Green. It was also played in the Kingstown Cricket Club on Adelaide Road. Swimming regattas were organised by the Royal St George Yacht Club. There was an active gymnasium at the Kingstown Men's Christian Institute. In August every year a junior sports day was held in the Royal Marine Gardens.

The Kingstown Bazaar was also held every August, in support of the local Catholic churches. The donations from the bazaar aimed to defray the cost of building churches at Monkstown and Glasthule, which were both completed in the mid-1860s. The fundraising began several years before the completion and continued for several years after. A feature of the bazaar was a monster raffle in which the prize was typically a piano or a grandfather clock.

LEISURE ON THE EAST PIER, c. 1860s

As Kingsdown was a seaside town, the regattas were the social events of the summer. The two early views on the left show fashionably dressed citizens or tourists on the East Pier. The first is marked 'Instantaneous' to indicate a camera type that became popular in the early 1860s. Both views show the lifeboat house (1861) and both appear to have an artistic quality. They date from different years, however, as a platform known as a dolphin is shown in one and the other photo appears to show rocks at that same point.

VICTORIA WHARF AND THE PAVILION, c. 1905

The Pavilion was built in 1903. When this picture was taken, the gardens had recently been planted but the tennis courts had not yet been laid. A close-up of the building shows the grand style and the sheer quantity of glass. The overall impression seems similar to that of the grand Mississippi river boats of the period.

The architects were Kaye-Parry and Ross, with Charles A. Owen. The builders were McLaughlin and Harvey and the gardens were laid out by William Sheppard.

PAVILION, JUNE, 1905

The Pavilion commenced construction in early 1903 and was completed and opened before Christmas of that year. It epitomised the grand aspirations of the socialites of the town. It included a large multipurpose grand hall, which could be used for balls, concerts, theatre, early cinema, and so on. It also included restaurants, smoking rooms, a bar, gardens, tennis courts, and mini golf. The design was striking, with much glass.

Later, the Pavilion had two major fires and was transformed over a period into a cinema. The site now includes retail shops, a bar, and a modern theatre called the Pavilion.

INSIDE THE PAVILION

Viennese balls were regular features there, with concerts in the early afternoon. Bioscopes, a primitive form of short silent movies, were a big craze when the Pavilion opened and almost every night ended with a showing. Examples of other entertainments were:

28 April 1904   Herr Krandt's famous Viennese Band

25 August 1904   Ashtons famous White Viennese Band under the direction of Andrew Krammer
    Hyden Opera Singers
    Animated pictures

26 September 1904 'The Follies' together with bioscope pictures including the consecration of the Cathedral in Armagh

17 October 1904   The Dale's Opera Singers and a programme of bioscope pictures

4 November 1904   MacNaghtens Renowned Vaudeville Company including:
    Harry Tate and his motor car (sketch)
    Fatmah Diard, the celebrated soprano
    Alber and Amber, wonderful American Comedy Jugglers
    Carne Curre and his educated dog
    Reilly and Taylor, comedians
    Japanese sleight of hand by Max Sterling
    Arthur Aldridge, tenor
    Pallisters American Bioscope
    Pavilion Grand Orchestra

Prices for these entertainments ranged from sixpence to two shillings. The newspapers frequently reported that audiences were 'fair', especially on the early days of the week.

TOWN HALL AND RAILWAY STATION, C. 1893

The Town Hall was designed by John Loftus Robinson and came into use in 1880. The Crofton Road entrance shows the word 'Courthouse'. If it was so used, it must have been only for a short time. The courthouse of the town for many years was located on Upper George's Street close to the DMP Barracks.

Visible in front of the Town Hall is the Dalkey Horse Tram. The Kingstown to Dalkey Horse Tram started on 19 March 1879 with a narrow-track gauge of 4ft. When the horse tram service from Dublin to Kingstown commenced in August 1885, it had a much wider gauge of 5ft 3in, similar to the Irish railways. So the Dalkey trams were incompatible with the city trams. The changeover point was at the Town Hall, where passengers from Dublin to Dalkey were obliged to change trams.

TOWN HALL SUNFLOWER MINSTRELS CONCERT, 25 APRIL 1892

The Town Hall was not just the seat of local government. It was the prime entertainment venue until the development of the Pavilion in 1903. It hosted balls, concerts, and meetings. It fostered local talent, which seems to have been there in abundance. A regular Friday night feature in 1892 was a concert given by a local amateur drama group, The Sunflower Minstrels from Blackrock. These amateurs managed to produce a different programme each week, using mostly the same performers. Clearly, they were a dedicated bunch.

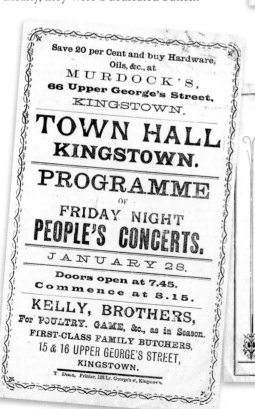

TOWN HALL PEOPLE'S CONCERT, 28 JANUARY 1898

In this 1898 concert, there is no indication of the affiliation of the performers to any association, club, or group. Indeed, there is no reference to amateur status.

The cinematograph, an early form of combined movie camera and projector, arrived in Kingstown three years after it was first produced by the Lumière brothers in France.

THE TREACY FAMILY

For about twenty years, the names of the Treacy brothers, Arthur Charles Treacy (1872–?) and Ernest Butler Treacy (1877–1955), kept popping up on entertainment shows of all types in the Town Hall and in other venues in the area. They were sons of Simon Treacy who lived at 5 Gresham Terrace in 1901. By 1911, Simon was not listed in the census, but Arthur had set up a business as electrical and general engineer at 3a Lower George's Street. The business continued until the 1950s, and Ernest's address at date of his death was given as the business address.

From 1899 onwards, Arthur was performing comic songs, and Ernest was stage manager for the concerts, known as Kingstown Popular Concerts, every alternate Saturday during the season. Arthur also appeared as a member of the Sunflower Minstrels of Blackrock in regular performances in Kingstown Town Hall.

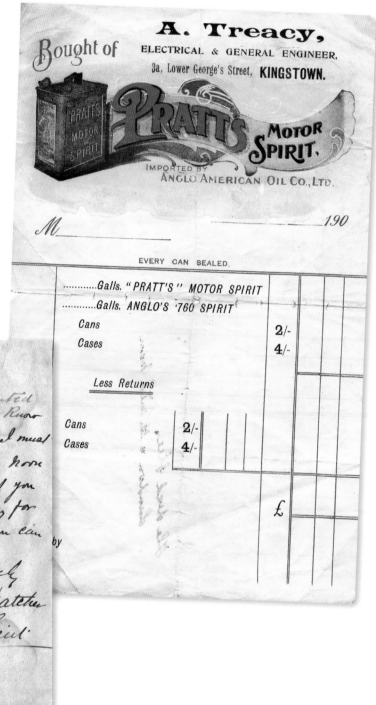

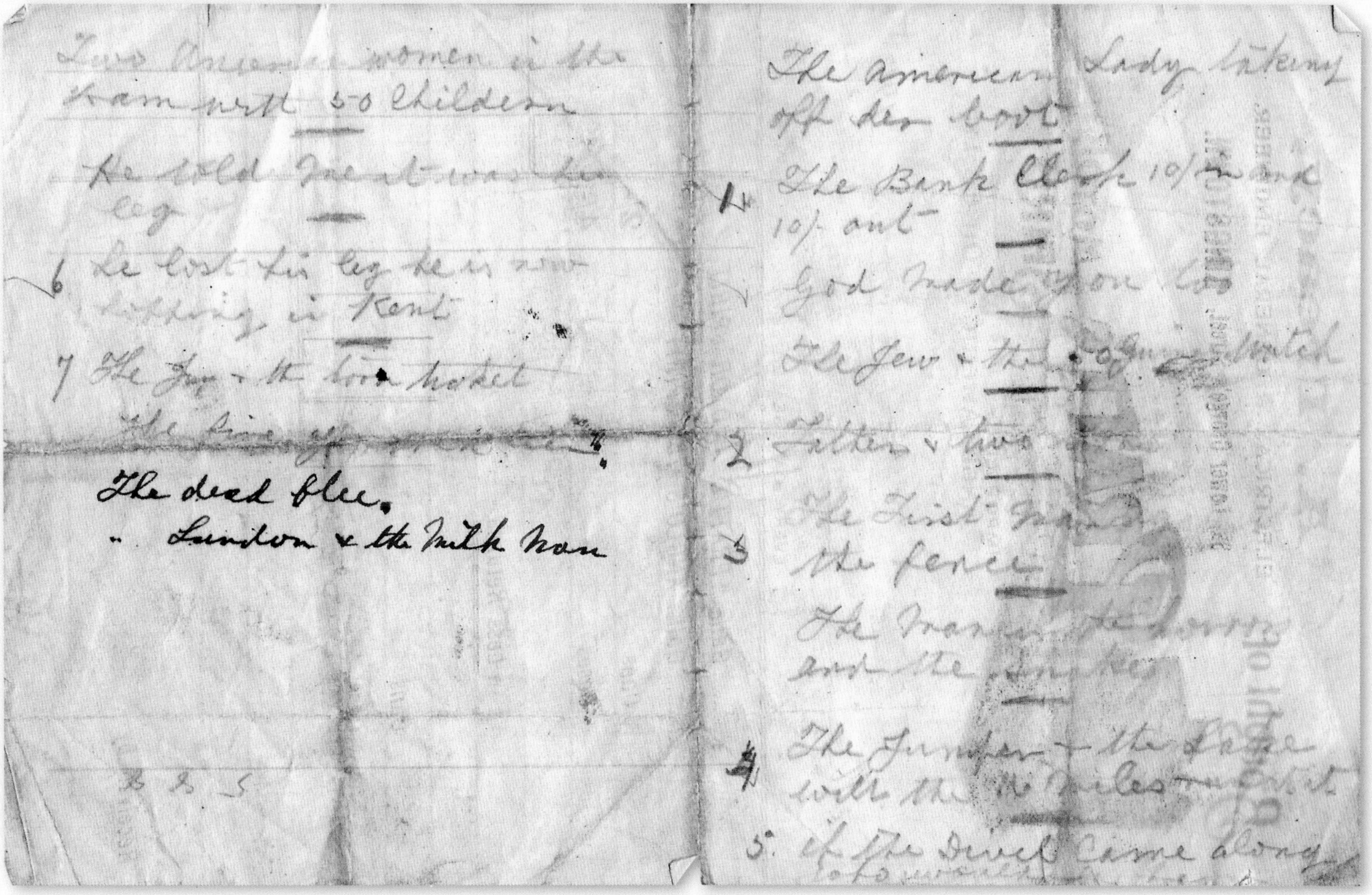

Two American women in the tram with 50 children

6 He lost his leg he is now hopping in Kent

7 The Jew & the [illegible] ticket

The dead flee.

.. Lindon & the Milk Man

The American Lady taking off her boot

1 The Bank Clerk 10/- in and 10/- out

God made [illegible]

The Jew & the [illegible] watch

2 [illegible]

3 The First [illegible] the fence

The Man [illegible] and the [illegible]

4 The Jumper & the [illegible] with the [illegible]

5 If the Devil came along

On Tuesday 12 June 1904, Lieutenant James O'Hatcher of the guardship HMS *Melampus* wrote to one of the Treacys asking for a concert to be organised on the following Tuesday (19 June) as part of an 'at home' for the petty officers and crew. An examination of the newspapers for any reference to such concert shows that on the day following the issuance of the letter, Thomas Gilleran, aged 24, a private on board HMS *Melampus*, was killed in a particularly gruesome accident at Athlone railway station. Gilleran and a comrade named Clarke were carrying on pranks on the platform while under the influence of drink when both fell on to the track. Clarke escaped. It is not known whether the 'at home' took place. The letter on Melampus notepaper is shown on the left.

Both of the Treacy brothers were involved in the engineering business. A couple of letterheadings from the business survive, and both of them have notes related to performances on the back.

The Treacy invoice shows that they stocked motor spirit (petrol) in sealed cans or cases, before petrol pumps arrived. A deposit ensured the return of the can or case. The back of this invoice has draft notes for a concert programme.

A later blank invoice from Treacy's shows a very wide range of services available for the car, motorcycle, boat, shop and home. On the back are the words of a song. The song has been identified as 'Down Among the Sugar-Cane' (1908) written by Avery & Hart, composed by Cecil Mack and Chris Smith.

The pantomime of 6 to 10 December 1909 is a great example of local initiative. The script and songs were entirely written by Ernest Treacy, and he played the lead part of the Widow Twankey. The full cast is shown in the programme, and in the picture below.

Repairs of Motor Launches,
Cars and Cycles.
All Sundries Stocked.
Nickelling, Enamelling, Forging,
Turning and Brazing.
Electric Bells and Speaking Tubes
supplied and fitted.
All Shops and House Fittings
supplied and repaired.
Motor Spirit, Grease, Paraffin,
Lubricating and Lighting
Oils, Carbide, &c., &c.

191

M

A. TREACY.

ELECTRICAL AND GENERAL ENGINEER,
3a LOWER GEORGE'S STREET, KINGSTOWN.

Programme.

DRAMATIS PERSONÆ.

King of Rundalee (Monarch of an unknown clime)
- - - Mr. Alfred Hand

King's Chief (He who assists the King to climb)
- - - Mr. M. O'Kelly

King's Jester (He who makes you forget the condition of the climate)
- - - Mr. V. O'Connor

Flower Girl (She who makes you love the climate)
- - - Miss Bab O'Brien

Demon (Evil Spirit of the clime) -
- - - Mr. P. J. Storm

Shepherd Boy - - -
- - - Miss Vesta Lynn

Princess - - -
- - - Miss Phyllis McGrath

DRAMATIS PERSONÆ.—Continued.

Fairy Queen (She who, by Magic-wand can Climatise)
- - - Miss Milly Kelly

Imp (He, who has nearly ceased to climb)
- - - Master T. O'Kelly

Silly Billy and Billy Treacle (They Who Wall-o in the Clime)
- Mr. Alf. Treville
- Mr. J. McWade

Widow Twankey (The Antique of the clime)
- - - Mr. Ernest Treacy

Cat (She who is quite accustomed to climb)
- - - Mr. Alf Treville

Villagers—Miss Marion Kelly, Miss Alice Kelly, Miss Kathleen Storey, Miss B. O'Brien, Miss Sophie Long, Mr. George Whitten, Mr. Thomas Elliott, Mr Herbert Cantillion, Mr. Edward Long, Mr. Stephen Colman.
Chorus of Villagers, Citizens, Courtiers, Fairies, Imps, etc.

SWIMMING REGATTAS

Swimming in salt-water baths or in the open sea were popular activities in this seaside town. There were open baths at Blackrock, Salthill, Kingstown, and Sandycove. Each had its own swimming club. Swimming was important for public health in a town where the basic hygiene facilities of water and sewers were defective and inadequate.

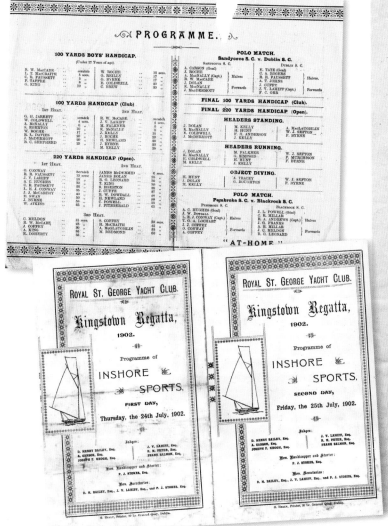

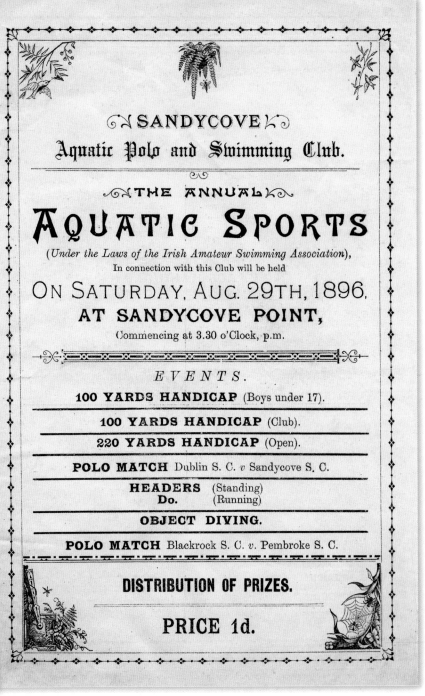

HOUSING IN KINGSTOWN

HOUSING IN KINGSTOWN

The houses of the wealthier merchants were located outside the town centre. A typical example is Alderley, one of the houses of the Tedcastle family, on the junction of Upper Glenageary Road and Adelaide Road. It was one of a line of elegant houses along that section of the road. The houses in the next section of Upper Glenageary Road were even grander, with much more extensive grounds.

Today, Alderley is divided into two houses, both of which are quite large by modern standards. The back portion of the house is now known as Eagle Lodge.

HOUSING IN KINGSTOWN 2

Many of the wealthier citizens of Dublin had a second home in Kingstown. Rosetta, on the Eastern end of the town was the second home of Mr William Fry, solicitor, who died in early 1906 aged 84. Fry was a native of Athlone and had offices and a residence at 13 Lower Mount Street, where he died. *Thom's Directory* shows that he owned Rosetta for more than thirty years. The legal firm of William Fry, solicitors, which he founded, is one of the largest legal firms in Dublin today.

The house was located at the end of Breffni Road, a prime seashore site on the corner as you turn in towards Bullock Harbour. The water laps up to the end of the garden, and the camera position must have been very close to the high water mark. Bullock Castle and Bullock Harbour are within 200m.

The large house has a plain design and dates from the earlier part of the 1800s.

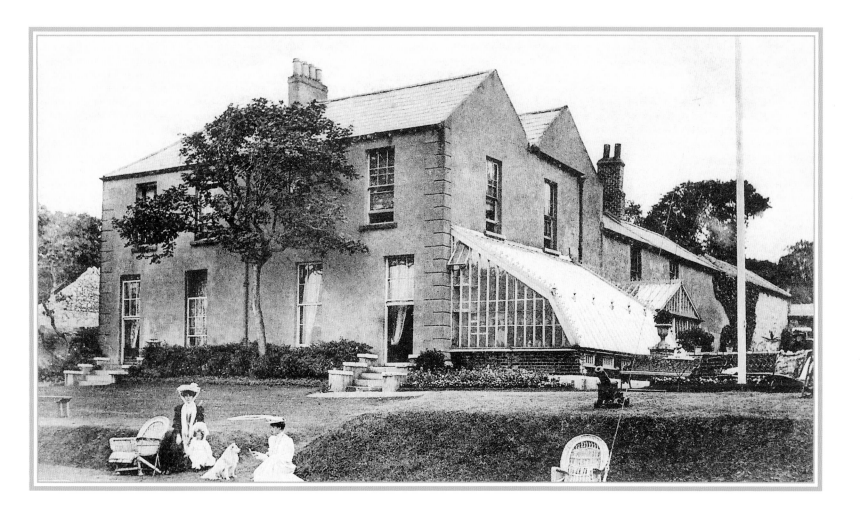

LONGFORD TERRACE AND TULLY'S ROW

Longford Terrace, Monkstown (right) is a set of twenty-eight houses in two terraced blocks of Victorian buildings of exceptional quality facing on to the railway and the sea. The older block, at the western end of the terrace, dates from the early 1840s. The newer block, shown prominently in the picture on the right, was built more than a decade later. This photo, part of a stereoview from about 1865, was taken from the grounds of Salthill Hotel, which was greatly extended about that time.

In the 1901 census more than half of the households are living on dividends, annuities, and rents. The legal profession is dominant among the working residents.

Part of the original village of Dunleary was a group of small houses called Tully's Row. The pathway in this picture of Longford Terrace is what remained after Tully's Row was demolished in the late 1850s or early 1860s. Maps of the late 1850s show about ten small houses on the north side of Tully's Row, in the area of the foreground of the picture.

HOUSING OF THE POORER CLASSES

There are very few photographs of the housing of the poorer classes in Kingstown/Dún Laoghaire. This one (left), taken sometime after 1923, shows Long's Row in Glasthule, with Devitt Villas in the background. Long's Row was subsequently demolished about 1934 to make way for Dixon's Villas.

There were eight houses in Long's Row in 1901. All were classified as third-class houses, on a scale of one to four. However, the detailed records show that two of them might have been more correctly classified as second class. These houses had solid walls and a good roof. Each house had two fireplaces. Six of them had two rooms, and two had three rooms. Many of the houses described in later chapters in this book were distinctly inferior to those in Long's Row.

STYLE IN KINGSTOWN

With an active social scene, style becomes an important facet of life. The wealthy citizens of the town had easy access by train to the best shops of Dublin, but could also take the boat from the Carlisle Pier in the morning and be in the shops of Knightsbridge or Regent Street the same evening.

STYLE AT NO. 6 VESEY PLACE

Vesey Place is a mid-Victorian terrace of large two-storey, double-fronted houses overlooking a private park. The 1901 census shows Joseph Alex Hayes, brewery manager, as the resident.

In August 1903, Commander Arthur Shirley and his wife were photographed there with Mrs Hugh Chafy and a Miss Chafy. The Chafys were relatives of the Shirleys. Two photos were taken in the garden. The first shows the three ladies beside a gazebo in the back garden.

The second picture shows, from the left: Miss Chafy, Mrs Shirley, Commander Shirley, and Mrs Hugh Chafy. The ladies are obviously dressed for a special occasion.

STYLE FOR CHILDREN

STUDIO PHOTOGRAPHS AT KINGSTOWN

When Queen Victoria came to Kingstown in 1900, the chairman of the urban district, Thomas W. Robinson, received a knighthood. The photograph below depicts his daughter, May, taken on that day at the door of the Town Hall was published as a stereoview and widely sold in the United States. May was the eldest of three children of the Robinson family who lived at 12 Clarinda Park North. Sir Thomas W. Robinson (1865–1946) was the Robinson partner of Hayes, Conyngham and Robinson pharmacies. Later, he held directorships for many of Dublin's best-known companies, including the Metropole Hotel, Millar and Beatty Ltd, Williams and Woods, and United Drug Company Ltd.

Above are two early cartes-de-visite by E.M. Cornwell at his studio at 83 Upper George's Street. The lady's name is not known. Cornwells was there about 1880.

The unknown gentleman on the left was photographed at the studios of H.D. Brown at 75 Lower George's Street. Brown was at this address in the early 1860s, but had moved before 1868 to No. 78. The picture therefore dates from the early 1860s.

The frockcoat with small lapels was popular in the early 1860s, as were the linen trousers and the large hat. The hats were normally made of felt and coloured black or brown, but this white one cuts quite a dash.

Boater hats were clearly popular when this carte-de-visite was taken at Clarendons at 94 Lower George's Street. In 2015, this shop is operated by Eduventure Ltd, but older natives will remember it as Doyles. Clarendons were there from the early 1860s through to the turn of the century and beyond. The date is not easily determined.

The obverse side of this carte-de-visite provides a date of Christmas 1901 and an address of Charleville. The photographer was Edward Bradford of Dalkey.

Charleville is a large house on Harbour Road, beside St Patrick's Church. The 1901 census indicates that the occupier was Foy Riviere, a wine merchant of Huguenot origin, but no person matching the description of this lady is listed.

PHOTOGRAPHERS AT KINGSTOWN

Kingstown had its share of photographers. Charles Cook was based in the town centre on Upper George's Street, facing Marine Road. Some of his postcards and pictures are reproduced elsewhere in this book. Some of his photographs are signed C. Neville Cook.

Three photographers in Lower George's Street, Browns, E.M. Cornwells, and Clarendons, offered cartes-de-visite. Bradfords of Dalkey also offered this service. The carte-de-visite was a photograph in a standard size, about the size of a credit card. They were cheap and could be used as a visiting card. These photographers also provided a full range of other sizes.

EDUCATION IN KINGSTOWN

Kingstown had a full range of schools, academies, and other places of learning. A detailed history of schools in the area is provided in Peter Pearson's *Between the Mountains and the Sea: Dún Laoghaire–Rathdown County* (O'Brien Press, 2007).

DOMINICAN CONVENT

The Dominican nuns came to Kingstown in 1847 and established themselves in Echo Lodge, a house donated to them by a Mrs Daly. The boarding school closed in 1971 and the secondary school in 1991 but the primary school is still in operation. This picture shows a junior class of 1892.

It appears that some form of craftwork was being taught, and the girls are displaying their handiwork, consisting mainly of dolls and a carriage for a doll. One of the girls is holding a small racket, possibly an early badminton racket.

The uniforms are in a variety of styles and were probably made by local dressmakers to a specified colour.

CBC EBLANA

The Christian Brothers College at Eblana
Avenue opened in 1856 and closed in 1992.

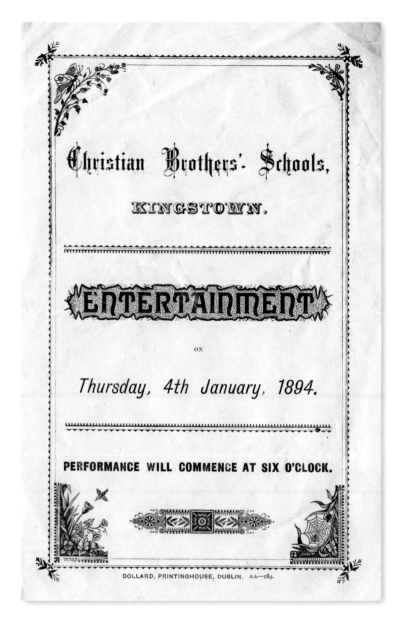

Two programmes for musical entertainments show quite different headings.
In 1893, the concert is labelled as 'Christian Schools'. The performers appear
to be the members of staff or other people, all using the title 'Mr'. One year
later, the show is labelled as 'Christian Brothers Schools' and the performers
include many pupils, as well as the people from the previous concert.

LORETO ABBEY AND CONVENT, DALKEY

Loreto Abbey in Dalkey opened its doors as a school for girls in 1843. The convent was designed by the foundress, Frances Ball, who acted as her own architect. It is now a fee-paying secondary school. The convent building has been well preserved, and the newer school buildings have been developed behind it.

HOLLYVILLE PARK SCHOOL, MONKSTOWN

Located at 3 Carrickbrennan Road, Monkstown, from about 1860–1890, Hollyville Park was advertised as 'a school for the sons of gentlemen'. It was a private school, with both boarders and day-pupils. It had a very wide curriculum of studies, including classical and modern languages, various branches of science, art, business, and economics. Religious classes were provided by the Church of Ireland, directly across the road.

The school had its own cricket team and regularly played against Trinity College, which suggests that boys may have continued to study there beyond the normal school leaving age.

Later, the schoolhouse became the property of Helen M. Goggin, wood carver, who was an internationally recognised sculptor in bog oak.

The schoolhouse building, which still retains much of its original architecture, was sold in 2015.

The above photo of the cricket pitch at Hollyville is interesting. It appears to date from about 1864 and is taken with a long lens from quite a distance, from the window of one of the houses at the top of Richmond Hill. The back of the school is visible in the centre of the picture, but the dominating feature is Monkstown Church of Ireland, towering over the school. The cricket pitch is now occupied by modern houses at Richmond Green and by the Oliver Plunkett National School.

Railways in and around Kingstown

Railways were an important part of the development of Kingstown. The first railway in Ireland was the Dublin-Kingstown railway, which started operations in 1834. The original terminus was closer to Salthill than to the present-day Dún Laoghaire (Mallin) station. The city terminus was at Westland Row.

The original line was laid on granite blocks longitudinally, but this proved unsatisfactory. When the line was relaid, shortly afterwards, and extended to the location of the present-day station, wooden sleepers were used. This may have been the first use of wooden sleepers on a railway.

The line was extended to Dalkey in 1843 as the atmospheric railway. It used a stationary engine at Dalkey to create a vacuum in a pipe beneath the train. A plunger in the vacuum pipe was attached to the train to pull it to Dalkey. The return journey was downhill and used gravity alone.

With the removal of the atmospheric line, the railway was extended southwards, reaching Bray (1854), Wicklow (1855), Enniscorthy (1863), and Wexford (1874). Attempts were made to extend the line northwards and to interconnect with other railways, including the construction of a railway tunnel under the Liffey in 1866, but all failed and it was not until 1891 that the loop line was constructed over the Liffey to connect the line to the rest of the railway network.

RAILWAY SIDING, GEORGE IV MONUMENT, AND CARLISLE PIER, c. 1890

When the Carlisle Pier was opened in 1859, a railway spur to deliver passengers directly to the dockside was a feature of the development. The service was provided by a short spur from the main railway line. Since the mainline railway was already in a cutting, a short tunnel was required. The tunnel, now disused, emerges just beside the premises of the Genealogical Society of Ireland. A level crossing just outside the tunnel brought the train in a curved line on to the actual pier. Although the line through the tunnel was single track, an additional track and turntable were required on the pier to facilitate turning the engine for the return journey. Maps of the 1860s show the booking office at the far end of the pier, but it was later moved to the near end.

The trains were scheduled to match the times of the mail boats, so that one could arrive at Westland Row station in the city centre half an hour before sailing time and be sure to catch the boat.

RAILWAY ON THE CARLISLE PIER, c. 1900

Compared with the previous picture, the significant change is the introduction of a railway signal. The mail boat has just arrived and passengers are coming down the platform while the luggage is being wheeled out by a porter. The jarvey with his sidecar is waiting for a fare.

RAILWAY AT SALTHILL

This carte-de-visite from about the mid–1860s shows the Salthill station, designed by Mulvany. A curious feature of the time is that although there were five footbridges over the line between Kingstown and Blackrock, there was none at the station.

There was, however, a footbridge over the railway at the nearby Salthill Hotel. This footbridge took hotel guests over the railway to the beach.

RAILWAY TRAGEDY 1867, BRAY HEAD

On 9 August 1867, shortly after 9 a.m., the 6.30 train from Enniscorthy was coming slowly towards Bray Head. In those days, the line crossed a ravine called Brandy Hole by way of a wooden viaduct. The line has since been moved further inland. The train crashed through the bridge barrier and the engine with some of the carriages plunged downwards. Two people were killed, and twenty-three were injured. The accident was attributed to faults in the laying of the track, rather than in the bridge. The report in the *Freeman's Journal* states that the line was repaired in time for the late train from Enniscorthy that evening.

HOSPITALS IN KINGSTOWN

There was a 'Lying-in Hospital' at 88 Lower George's Street from about 1850. The present (2016) incumbent of the site is the constituency office of People Before Profit, a political party.

In the late 1860s, the Sisters of Mercy were asked by Very Revd Canon McCabe, parish priest of Kingstown, to establish a hospital in the town. They responded by opening a temporary hospital in Pakenham Road, Monkstown, in a 'small, ill-ventilated, close, and inconvenient house and grounds', and making arrangements for a larger hospital to be built. Charitable donations were invited towards the building of the new hospital.

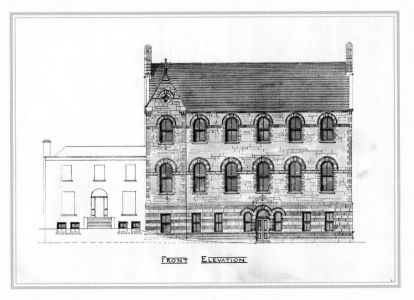

FRONT ELEVATION

The site chosen, at No. 100 Lower George's Street, was that of a large house (two-storey over basement) called Harrymount, which was set well back from the building line of the street. For the previous twenty years, Harrymount had been the Town Hall, including the offices of the Town Commissioners. The contract plans, dated 19 November 1874, show Harrymount retained as an annexe to the new hospital. The architect was John Loftus Robinson. The builder was Michael Meade & Co. Robinson and Meade later collaborated on the new Town Hall (c. 1870).

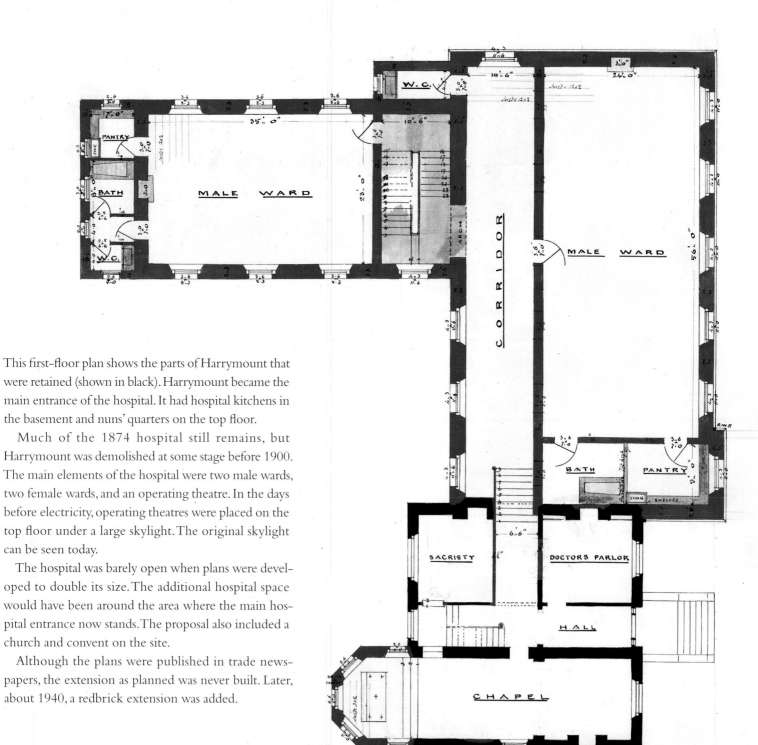

This first-floor plan shows the parts of Harrymount that were retained (shown in black). Harrymount became the main entrance of the hospital. It had hospital kitchens in the basement and nuns' quarters on the top floor.

Much of the 1874 hospital still remains, but Harrymount was demolished at some stage before 1900. The main elements of the hospital were two male wards, two female wards, and an operating theatre. In the days before electricity, operating theatres were placed on the top floor under a large skylight. The original skylight can be seen today.

The hospital was barely open when plans were developed to double its size. The additional hospital space would have been around the area where the main hospital entrance now stands. The proposal also included a church and convent on the site.

Although the plans were published in trade newspapers, the extension as planned was never built. Later, about 1940, a redbrick extension was added.

DEATH IN KINGSTOWN, c. 1865

Before the opening of Deansgrange Cemetery in 1865, the cemetery at St Fintan's, Kill o' the Grange, was used for burials. The records of burials at St Fintan's are missing but some of the tombstones have survived and can provide us with names and dates.

The picture below is half of a stereoview from the 1860s, which was sold in the US, presumably to remind emigrants of their homeland. When viewed using Victorian stereoview apparatus, these panels provide an extraordinary three-dimensional ghoulish picture. The National Library of Ireland has another stereoview from the same cemetery.

Enlargement of the grave marker of Mick Dowdel, d. 28 May 1863. Mick was probably a modest man of little means and limited education. His wooden cross would have disappeared soon after, and with it, all trace of his existence, except for this photograph.

The church ruin and the cemetery at St Fintan's have been cleaned up. This operation included the removal of the large tree that had grown up through the nave of the church. Two of the gravestones from the earlier picture have survived.

DUNLARY, DUNLEARY, KINGSTOWN, DÚN LAOGHAIRE, DUNLAOIRE - WHAT'S IN A NAME?

The earliest written records of the village show the name Dunleary or Dunlary, a name derived from the Irish (Gaelic) words meaning Fort of Laoghaire. The fort is reputed to have been located in the vicinity of the Battery Bridge on Crofton Road. Laoghaire was a High King of Ireland in the fifth century AD.

King George IV embarked from the town on 3 September 1821, at the close of his visit to Ireland, and the name Kingstown was applied to the town in honour of his visit. The name change was effective immediately and was used in news reports in the *Freeman's Journal* three days later.

Not everybody was happy with the name Kingstown. Hugh Byrne, writing in the *Irish People* on 23 January 1864 in a lengthy piece entitled 'Kingstown Nomenclature', stated that 'the very name of Kingstown, which should be New Dunleary, and the names of hundreds of places in it, tell a painful story of national servitude, public debasement, and individual pedantry, ignorance, and flunkeyism'. He suggested names such as Emmet Place, Wolfe Tone Avenue, and Benburb Road. Had he lived long enough, he would have seen Wolfe Tone Avenue in Dún Laoghaire and Emmet Street in Sallynoggin. His article was republished in the *Irish Nation* on 23 February 1883, which may have given rise to the Robinson initiative on this subject just three years later.

On 1 March 1886, John Loftus Robinson brought forward a motion to the Kingstown Township Board to change the name from Kingstown to Old Dunleary. After some discussion the motion was withdrawn by the proposer 'until a board more conversant with national principles was in office'. The item was carried by the *Freeman's Journal* on 2 March and by the *Irish American Weekly* on 27 March.

From the 1880s onwards, local sporting and cultural organisations with nationalist leanings were increasingly using the name 'Dunleary' in their names, and branches of national organisations were titled 'Dunleary Branch'. There was a Dunleary GAA tournament each year in the late 1880s and in the 1890s. The Dunleary Branch Irish National Foresters regularly had dances in the Town Hall in the 1890s. Connradh na Gaedhilge had a Dunleary men's branch and a Dunleary ladies' branch. There was Dunleary Cumann na nGaedheal from 1902 and Dunleary Division (A693) AOH (Ancient Order of Hibernians). There was a Dunleary Feis in the Town Hall each year from about 1905, and a Dunleary Gaelic League about 1911. In 1920 there was Dunleary United Irish League.

On 6 July 1920, at a meeting of the Kingstown Urban District Council, a motion was proposed by Seán Ó hUadhaigh, solicitor and councillor, to change the name of the town to Dún Laoghaire. Two days later, the *Irish Independent* carried the news with the headline 'Back to the old name– Dunleary replaces "Kingstown".'

Ó hUadhaigh was not pleased with this headline and the subsequent reports. He wrote to several newspapers and they published his letter:

A Chara,

As one who has had some share in the recent alteration of the name of 'Kingstown' to 'Dún Laoghaire', which only awaits the sanction of Dublin County Council and the publication of certain notices to become legally binding, permit me to appeal to the public and to the Press to preserve the proper spelling of the name of the town. I would not personally like to be responsible for altering the name 'Kingstown', objectionable as it is to our National pride, if it, which is at least good English, were to be substituted by an incorrect form of the Irish name. The Council has not re-named the town 'Dunleary', which represents the half-hearted effort of some planter to vocalize the old name, but 'Dún Laoghaire'. It is inconsistent with National dignity for us Irish to adapt our place-names and our National system of phonetics to suit foreigners or those who ape them at home. For the benefit of those whose sympathies with 'Irish ideas' are larger than their acquaintance with our National language may I point out that the correct pronunciation of the restored title (as near as one can get in English equivalents) 'Dhoon Layer-a' or 'Dhoon Lair-a', the final 'a' being just as it is pronounced in the words 'a man' or 'a dog'.

– Mise do chara,

On 7 August 1920 the following advertisement appeared in the *Freeman's Journal*:

URBAN DISTRICT OF DÚN LAOGHAIRE

(Formerly Urban District of Kingstown)

NOTICE OF CHANGE OF NAME

WHEREAS at a duly convened Meeting of the Council of the Urban District of Kingstown, held on the 6th day of July, 1920, a Resolution was passed that the Kingstown Urban District Council change their name and style and the name of their district to the Dún Laoghaire Urban District Council and the Dún Laoghaire Urban District respectively.

AND WHEREAS at a meeting of the Dublin County Council held on the 24th day of July, 1920, the proposed changes of the names of the said Urban District Council and District Council respectively were duly sanctioned by the said County Council.

Now NOTICE IS HEREBY GIVEN that the names heretofore borne by the said Urban District Council and Urban District respectively shall be abandoned and that the said Urban District Council and Urban District shall from henceforth be known as and called by the names of the Dún Laoghaire Urban District Council and the Dún Laoghaire Urban District Council respectively.

Dated the 5th day of August, 1920

Town Hall J. SHERLOCK VAUGHAN,

Dún Laoghaire Town Clerk

Co Dublin

Some references to the name Kingstown remained. Separate legal processes were required to change the name of the harbour and the railway station, and these took some time.

According to Brian Scott on page 46 of his publication *Sealink and its predecessors in Dublin* (Dublin, 1989): 'On the 2nd of December 1920 a Traffic Conference meeting in London acknowledged the change of the name from Kingstown'. This acknowledgement sorted the problem of the railway station. In respect of the harbour, the name change was facilitated by the Section 10 of the State Harbours Act, 1924.

Many local businesses and organisations, including sporting clubs, had the name Kingstown as part of their name. Most changed within a short period of time, but a number held out. The final organisation to use the name was probably the Kingstown Grammar School, later Avoca and Kingstown Grammar School, which retained the Kingstown element in its name until about 1972.

A Town of Contrasting Fortunes

'THE MOST ARISTOCRATIC SUBURB OF THIS CITY'

By the 1840s, the town of Kingstown had grown from a village to an important town. It now extended across hundreds of acres which only twenty-five years earlier had been unfenced common land, strewn with rocks.

With a regular fast railway service to Dublin city, it quickly became fashionable, as well as convenient, to commute from Kingstown to work in the city. Builders and developers moved rapidly to satisfy the demand by constructing whole rows of cottages terraces, houses, and villas. Large, and sometimes extravagant, mansions were built around the outskirts. Senior civil servants, doctors, engineers, and merchants came to live in the town.

There were others who did not take the train each morning. The census of 1901 would later show that a substantial number of residents of large houses were living on unearned income, such as dividends, annuities, and rents. Clearly, there was large accumulated wealth to support such a lifestyle. Such wealth was doubtless there throughout the Victorian period.

Churches were established by a wide range of Christian denominations in the town and in the surrounding area. Retailers along the main street provided for the needs of the most discerning shoppers. Similarly, cafés and drinking establishments catered for their refreshments. Yacht clubs were established along the seafront, and a line of hotels was built facing the harbour.

Kingstown had become predominantly a residential suburb. One Dublin newspaper of the time described it as 'the most opulent, most populous, and most aristocratic suburb of this [Dublin] city'.

'A CONSIDERABLE NUMBER [OF HOUSES] ARE BARELY FIT FOR HUMAN HABITATION'

Hidden deep within the historical record, and never photographed at the time, were the houses and the living conditions of those less fortunate in society. These dwellings have been all but obliterated or modified beyond recognition. Even the addresses that identified them have been eliminated. However, there are available records from that time that detail the circumstances of the poor. They tell a story of an under-class which comprised a large proportion of the population of the town, and which existed in overcrowded, sub-standard accommodation with little or no sanitary facilities. Cholera, tuberculosis, and other diseases ran rife.

What is most surprising is that with such levels of poverty, there were only a few areas where the poverty was concentrated. Instead, the poverty was widely spread in the town, in the most unlikely places. There is evidence of a large number of 'courts'. These courts were the backyards of houses and shops on the main streets. These backyards were fitted out with huts, sheds, and other primitive makeshift accommodation for whole groups of families. The evidence is that in many cases, the poor and the more affluent lived in very close proximity to each other along most of the main streets of the town.

The story of the poverty in Kingstown had its origins in the way that the town developed. The construction of the harbour required a small number of skilled engineers and overseers, but the bulk of the work was done by low-skilled or unskilled workers. After some years of rapid construction, the harbour project slowed and employment opportunities dried up. In the economic conditions of nineteenth-century Ireland, there was little opportunity for those workers to move on to alternative employment. Indeed, it is likely that unemployed workers from elsewhere might have been attracted to Kingstown as a place of apparent prosperity.

In the construction of the buildings of the town, priority was clearly given to the building of houses for the upper classes because this provided greater profits for the builders. In Dublin city, and in some towns, the natural course of events was that as the citizens became more affluent, they moved to better houses, leaving the older stock of houses for the poorer classes. This process sometimes created tenements. By the end of the Victorian period, there were about 300 tenement houses in Kingstown, which was quite a large number for a town of its size. But tenements alone were not nearly sufficient to accommodate the poor of the town.

Soon after the start of the development of the new town, makeshift sheds, huts, and outhouses began to be constructed as living accommodation in every available backyard. These were called courts, and each of the courts was given an address which was frequently the name of the lessor to whom the rent was payable. By 1849, there were large numbers of courts throughout the town. Ball's Court, Flynn's Court and Duff's Court are examples, all of which were located on or close to the site where the Carnegie Library was later built around 1912, at the junction of Library Road and Lower George's Street.

The lessors who collected rents from the courts appear to have been small-time operators. In many cases, they appear to have been the owners or lessees of street-fronting premises who had set up some sheds in the backyard. In other cases, the entire court, or a large portion of it, was registered in the name of one of the residents of the court, and in such cases he normally had a dwelling which was just slightly better than his neighbours. It is unclear whether some of those lessors were acting on their own behalf, or on behalf of the ultimate landlords of the area, the Lords Longford and de Vesci.

TRACKING THE POVERTY IN VICTORIAN KINGSTOWN

There are reliable extant indicators of poverty in nineteenth-century Kingstown. These records were compiled for administrative purposes or to throw light upon health-related issues. The Griffith's Valuation of 1849 and the censuses of 1901 and 1911 provide direct information on the housing stock. The Haliday/Madden report of 1867 and the Browne report of 1902 both provide measures of the sanitation facilities in these dwellings. The report of the evidence to the Taxation of Towns Inquiry Commission (Kingstown & Dalkey) 1877 also provides valuable insights into the state of housing and sanitation in the town.

These various reports indicate that more than one-third of the population lived in extreme poverty, in primitive cabin-type accommodation. A further large proportion lived in poor-quality tenements where multiple families might have one room each, possibly with shared use of a kitchen and/or a shared rudimentary toilet.

Shelter, clean water, and clean air are among the basic physiological need of society. The various reports indicate deprivation on some or all of these fronts. Invariably, these deprivations were accompanied by further deprivations not always recorded, such as food, clothing, and education.

THE GRIFFITH VALUATION, 1849

The Great Irish Famine, which raged through the Irish countryside from 1845, appears to have had a lesser effect upon Kingstown than upon more rural areas. Unlike in many parts of Ireland, the population continued to grow in Kingstown during this period. Indeed, it is likely that the population was swelled by poor unfortunates who may have moved there to avoid the worst ravages of the famine.

The famine was still in progress when the Griffith's Valuation of 1849 was undertaken in Kingstown. The valuation inspectors placed a value on every building or piece of land, and listed the name of the owner or lessor and lessee. Using the valuation lists, we can find the location and quality of the housing stock, including the poorest-quality housing.

The valuation lists show the addresses, and in some cases indicates the location, relative to a landmark such as a numbered shop on the main street. Flynn's Court, for example is listed as 'at rere of 28 George's St. Lr'. Griffith's Valuation shows forty-nine places using the title 'Court' in Kingstown, and a number of other locations with similar characteristics using names such as 'Lane'.

Dwellings were valued by reference to the potential rent which might be obtainable in the marketplace. It is safe to say that any dwelling which was assessed by the valuers at £3 was of very inferior quality. Typically, it would have flimsy walls, a primitive roof, a single room or two small rooms, and little else. A dwelling with a valuation of £5 would likely have a somewhat less fragile structure, but nothing by way of home comforts. The Appendix provides some details and locations of houses having valuations of £3 and £5 respectively.

THE HALIDAY REPORT, 1866

Charles Haliday was a businessman, historian, and rights campaigner who lived in Monkstown. A report by Haliday, which was unpublished at the time of his death in 1866 but was published shortly thereafter, clearly illustrates a level of squalor and insanitary conditions as well as the regular incidence of disease and infant mortality. He called for a range of improvements.

Six months later in a letter to the newspapers, Dr Thomas More Madden, together with his father Dr Richard Robert Madden, commenting on the Haliday report, expressed their frustration with the lack of progress. They called for the local authority to be set aside and to have these necessary improvements effected by competent officials appointed by and responsible to the government.

TAXATION OF TOWNS INQUIRY COMMISSION (KINGSTOWN AND DALKEY) 1877

This Royal Commission documented 128 pages of detailed evidence from thirty-two witnesses on the state of housing and sanitation in the town. Witnesses ranged from individual town commissioners through to the town clerk and his staff, local doctors, and interested parties.

THE CENSUS, 1901

The census of 1901 provides some extensive detail on the citizens of the town. It also provides considerable detail on the housing stock. For each street, road, court, or lane, a House and Building Return is available which classifies the quality of the individual houses and the number of rooms available to each family.

It shows extensive overcrowding in the courts and tenements, where most of the families have just one or two rooms.

There are, however, some doubts about the extent of reporting in the 1901 census. Some whole courts and lanes are missing from the records and were probably not recorded. In relation to those courts and lanes that were recorded, it appears likely that the incidence of poor-quality housing was under-reported.

THE BROWNE REPORT ON KINGSTOWN, 1902

The conditions of disease and sanitation in more than forty towns and cities in Ireland were reviewed by a panel of medical inspectors from the Local Government Board in 1900 and 1901 and published in 1902.

Dr T.J. Browne was asked to report on Kingstown. His report is a 10-page section of a 327-page document prepared by the Local Government Board for Ireland. Browne prepared reports for more than twenty towns.

His Kingstown report stands out as the most detailed of the more than forty reports and is the most damning. It details conditions of filth and squalor in the courts and lanes in all areas of the town. The Kingstown report covers much more than the sanitary facilities. It provides a view of housing conditions of the working classes.

Browne reports that there are 121 courts and laneways with:

1,007 houses of the poorer class. Nearly all of these houses are one-storey buildings, containing one or two rooms each, structurally defective, and, in many instances, in bad repair. A considerable portion are barely fit for habitation and many are quite unfit … The worst of these courts are to be found off Patrick Street, George's Street, Mulgrave Street, Cumberland Street, Cross Avenue, Paradise Street [now Convent Road] Clarence Street, Turners Avenue, and Callaghan's Lane.

Further, Browne reports that there are 355 tenement dwellings in the district:

> The slum property in Kingstown is of the worst description and fit for nothing except demolition … the leases of most of this class of property will expire in two or three years, when, in all probability, the houses, or a large number of them, will be demolished.

Among the matters most urgently demanding attention, Browne listed as his first priority 'The clearance of the worst slum areas and the provision of healthy dwellings for the working classes'.

The tenements referred to by Browne were a little different from those in the city centre. The generally accepted image of Dublin tenements is of terraces of very large three-storey or four-storey houses, usually over basements. Those houses were old and no longer suitable for the lifestyle of the original wealthy occupants for whom they had been constructed. By contrast, the tenement houses of Kingstown were smaller and not as old. Most likely, the dwellings to which Browne refers were smaller houses built very quickly in the first decade after the start of construction of the harbour, at a time when the quality of building may have been compromised in the interests of speed. As a tenement, such houses could produce a tidy rent if a separate family could occupy each room.

THE KINGSTOWN IMPROVEMENT SCHEME

As the twentieth century arrived, efforts began to be made to resolve the housing situation. The distinctive redbrick houses along Cumberland Street, Barrett Street, Cross Avenue, Mill's Street, Wolfe Tone Avenue, Desmond Avenue, and others were built and quickly occupied. Other developments followed, so that in a 1936 report commissioned and paid for by Dún Laoghaire Borough Corporation, Manning Robertson, an eminent town planner, felt able to report that 'Thanks to the efforts which have been made by the Corporation, the housing situation in Dún Laoghaire is unusually satisfactory'.

Improved housing does not eliminate poverty. It simply makes poverty more tolerable, and the effects of Victorian poverty in Kingstown remained for many years.

LOST ADDRESSES OF KINGSTOWN/DÚN LAOGHAIRE

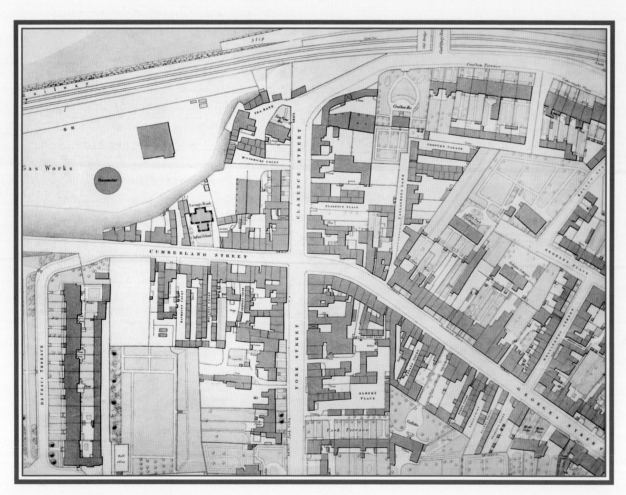

People searching for information about their ancestors in Kingstown/Dún Laoghaire are frequently confronted by addresses that they cannot locate. These were almost invariably the addresses of the dwellings of the poorest people of the town.

There is a very long list of so-called lost addresses. Many of the dwellings were demolished in the first decade of the twentieth century as part of the Kingstown Improvement Schemes, but some have remained right through to the early part of the twenty-first century.

A particular feature of the lost addresses was the fact that they were almost invariably cul-de-sacs. Some were entered through narrow gaps between houses; some others through archways or doorways on main streets or on alleyways. Either way, they were located in such a way that the more fortunate citizens of the town would not be required to walk through them, and would barely notice their existence in many cases. It was easy to turn a blind eye to them.

This list has been compiled from maps, directories, from the various reports covered in this book, and from other miscellaneous documents held by the author.

The 1866 map shows a large number of lost addresses in the western end of the town.

Cumberland Street and the surrounding area, 1866. Off Cumberland Street can be seen:

1   Baymount Court, on the site that is now part of Dún Laoghaire Further Education Institute. It is entered through an arch on Cumberland Street.
2   Molloy's Court and Sexton's Court, which were replaced by Barrett Street. Molloy's Court has a narrow arched entrance off Cumberland Street. The entrance to Sexton's Court is unclear.
3   Duff's Court, across the road, was approximately behind Nos 7 and 8 Cumberland Street.
4   Two other unnamed courts can be clearly seen on either side of Baymount Court.

Seven further courts not shown on this map are known to have been located off Cumberland Street and are shown in the list below.

McCormick's Court, off Clarence Street, was later replaced by a coalyard for many years. It is now the site of offices and apartments. It appears to have been entered through a narrow gate. At least four further courts not shown on this map are in the list below.

Off York Road (then named as York Street) was Albert Place, now the location of Nos 1 to 14 Smyth's Villas. Multiple other courts were located in this section but are not shown on the map.

Off Lower George's Street can be seen:

1   The entrance to Jones' Court, approximately in the present-day premises of Champs Barbers, almost opposite Gilbert and Wrights pub. The entrance is through a narrow doorway or arch.
2   Between Jones' Court and Fagan's Court, there is possibly another court, unnamed.
3   Fagan's Court, located behind the premises now occupied by Just Beds in Lower George's Street.
4   Burn's Court, later the location of the 1912 Carnegie Library. Later maps list this as Duff's Court.
5   Ball's Court, also on the 1912 Carnegie Library site.
6   Flynn's Court on which Library Road was constructed about 1912.
7   Bradley's Court, now Robert Downey Auctioneer's premises.

Multiple other courts in this section of Lower George's Street are unmarked.

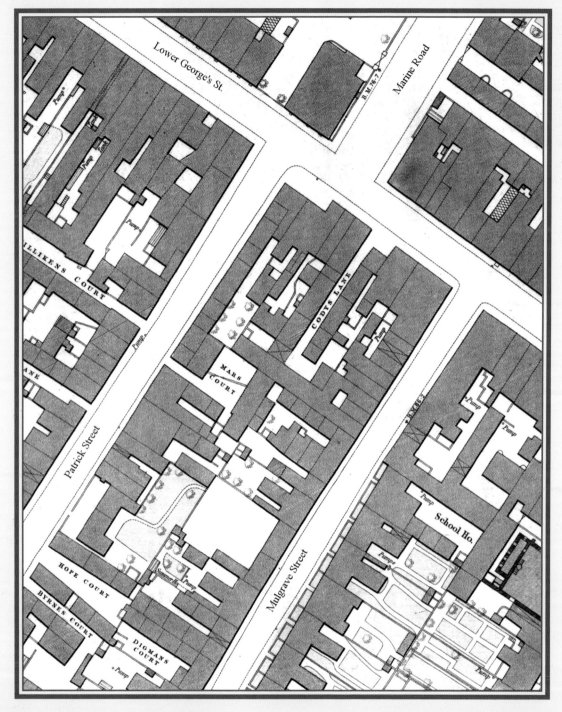

Courts Map 2 (left) shows part the area between Mulgrave Street and Patrick Street in 1866.

Cody's Lane, on Upper George's Street, was entered by way of a narrow lane between Nos 4 and 5 Upper George's Street. In 2015 terms, this lane is through the Blue Ginger restaurant. It should not be confused with Cody's Court, which was located at rear of No. 65 Kingstown Avenue, now Patrick Street.

Off Patrick Street are shown:

1 Milliken's Court, renamed in 2014 as Cantwell Lane. In the 1901 census, this court had twelve dwellings for fourteen families.
2 Pave Lane at its peak in 1867 had eighteen dwellings.
3 Mar's Court, occupying part of a lane renamed in 2014 as Lee's Lane.
4 Hope Court had four dwellings.
5 Byrne's Court was one of a number of courts of the same name.

Digman's Court, which was also cited as Dignam's Court, is marked off Mulgrave Street. There were two courts of this name on Mulgrave Street.

The following pages show a list of lost addresses compiled from a combination of reports, maps, directories and other sources for the Victorian period. It attempts to show the location, where possible, and in certain cases additional information such as the origin of the name.

The following abbreviations are used in this table:

GV   Griffith's Valuation

Thom's   *Thom's Directory* – published each year from the 1840s. Most references
            to *Thom's* in this table relate to the 1850, 1852, or 1893 editions

Haliday   *A Statistical Inquiry into the Sanitary Condition of Kingstown* – Charles
            Haliday 1866 – edited by Thomas More Madden, published by
            Fowler, Dublin 1867

Browne   *Report on the sanitary circumstances and administration of Kingstown
            Urban District* by Dr T. J. Browne, published as p.158 et seq of
            'Supplement to the twenty-ninth annual report of the Local Government
            Board for Ireland 1900-1' – HMSO 1902

Address	Location
Air Hill Avenue	Almost certainly located in the vicinity of Air Hill House, off York Street, which was later renamed York Road.
Albert Place	Located on the town side of York Street, later renamed York Road, between Nos 63 and 64, according to *Thom's*. It is now the location of Nos 1 to 14 Smyths Villas.
Anderson's Court	Located at the rear of 4 Wellington Place. The lessor is named as William Anderson, who also leased the main house. There is no record of his address.
Andrew's Court	Located beside 4 Wellington Street. It is now the premises of Waterloo Bathrooms.
Annamount	Located on Mulgrave Street.
Anglesea Cottages	Located on Upper George's Street, according to Browne.
Archbold's Court	Located on Patrick Street, according to Browne and *Thom's*. Jane Archbold is listed as the lessor of two of the dwellings and as the occupier in the third, according to GV.
Arde's Court AKA Airds Court AKA Arde's Cottages	Located at the rear of 20 Tivoli Avenue. Patrick Arde is listed as the lessor. He also leased Nos 21 and 22 Tivoli Avenue. He lived at 21 Tivoli Avenue, according to GV.
Ardnagreina	Believed to be located on Tivoli Road.
Atwell's Court AKA Atwool's Court	Located at the rear of Nos 1 and 2 Tivoli Avenue. William Atwell is listed as the lessor of these houses and of six houses in Tivoli Avenue, including Nos 1 and 2. He is also listed as lessor of eight small dwellings on Paradise Row. No person of that name is listed as an occupier in County Dublin.
Avoca Square AKA Ovoca Square	Located off the west side of York Road. It is now lost under Nos 20 to 32 Smyth's Villas.

Address	Location
Avondale	Located at the present position of O'Rourke Park, Sallynoggin.
Ball's Court	Located on Lower George's Street at Library Road. Ball's Court lies underneath the east walls of the Carnegie Library. Haliday lists it as sharing facilities with Nos 22 and 23 Lower George's Street.
Baxters Court	Located on Patrick Street, according to Browne and *Thom's* of 1850.
Baxters Lane	Believed to be located on Patrick Street.
Baylis Court	Located at the rear of Nos 17 and 18 Rumley Avenue, now Mulgrave Street. The lessor was Mrs Baylis who lived at Albert Road, Sandycove. This address is also listed as Dignam's Court in *Thom's* of 1893.
Baymount Court	Located through an archway next to 19 Cumberland Street. It was demolished and replaced by council houses.
Beatty's Court	Located on Turner's Avenue, off Cross Avenue, close to Wolfe Tone Avenue.
Beaumont Place	Not known.
Begg's Court	Located on Mulgrave Street.
Begg's Lane	Probably located on Mulgrave Street.
Bond's Cottages	Located in Lower Mountown.
Bond's Court	Located on Turner's Avenue, off Cross Avenue, close to Wolfe Tone Avenue.
Bond's Lane	Located off Turner's Lane or Paradise Place, off Cross Avenue, close to Wolfe Tone Avenue. Joseph Bond was the lessor of five dwellings here. He appears to have owned two houses, Nos 21 and 55, on York Road. He was also the lessor of a number of small properties in Kingstown and Monkstown.
Boyd's Court	Located in Thomastown, on the east side of Sallynoggin Road.
Boyle's Court	Not known.
Bradley's Lane AKA Bradley's Court	Located at the rear of 29 Lower George's Street, according to GV. *Thom's* of 1893 shows Bradley's Court at an entrance between Nos 22 and 23. Haliday lists it as sharing facilities with No. 25. William Bradley was the lessor and lived at 42 Northumberland Avenue.
Brazil's Court	Located on Mulgrave Street, according to Browne and *Thom's* of 1850.
Brewster's Cottages	Located off Corrig Avenue. Brewster's Cottages were located precisely at the car park entrance between the courthouse and an adjacent office block. It is shown but not named on the 1908 map and was still in existence until the 1960s.
Brian's Court	Located off Paradise Row, in the Convent Road area.

Address	Location
Brian's Court (2)	Located on Cross Avenue. Browne clearly indicates that there were two separate locations called Brian's Court, in close proximity to each other.
Brien's Court	Probably the same as one of the Brian's Courts above.
Bruce's Court	Located on Cumberland Street.
Bryan's Court	Probably the same as one of the Brian's Courts above.
Burne's Court AKA Byrne's Court	Located on Patrick Street.
Byrne's cottages	Located on Kelly's Avenue.
Byrne's Court	Located at the rear of 25 Lower George's Street, according to GV. Haliday lists it as sharing facilities with 21 Lower George's Street.
Byrne's Court	Located at the rear of number 64 Kingstown Avenue.
Byrne's Court	Located on Cumberland Street.
Byrne's Court	Not known. Haliday lists three places called Byrne's Court. This one does not seem to match with any other listed.
Byrne's Land	Located off No. 67 Kingstown Avenue.
Cambridge Place	Not known.
Carrig Court	Located off Corrig Avenue.
Carroll's Cottages	Located on Adelaide Road.
Carroll's Court	Located on Patrick Street.
Carroll's Court	Located on Crofton Avenue.
Castella Place	Located between Nos 44 and 45 York Street, later renamed York Road, according to the *Thom's* of 1852.
Chandler's Court	Located on York Street, later renamed York Road.
Clancy's Court	Located on York Street, later renamed York Road.
Clarence Place	Located at the narrow end of Callaghan's Lane. It was demolished to extend George's Place to meet with Clarence Street between Nos 3 and 4, according to *Thom's* of 1893 and the Ordnance Survey of Ireland (OSI).
Clarke's Court	Located on Lower George's Street, according to Browne. The Clarke family lived in No. 1 around 1901.
Clarke's Court	Located on Cumberland Street.
Codd's Lane AKA Codd's Court	Located on George's Street, according to Haliday. John Codd lived in No. 3 and was lessor of No. 4.
Cody's Court	Located at the rear of No. 65 Kingstown Avenue. Denis Cody lived at No. 65 Kingstown Avenue and is listed as lessor of these dwellings. It was indexed online as Cady's Court on the 1901 census although the handwritten returns clearly state Cody's Court. It should not be confused with Cody's Lane which was entered at number 5 Upper George's Street and is now the Blue Ginger Restaurant.

Address	Location
Connolly's Court	Located on Cumberland Street.
Connor's Court	Located at the rear of Nos 14 and 15 Rumley Avenue, now Mulgrave Street. James Connor was the lessor of all nine dwellings. 15 Rumley Avenue was occupied by 'James Connor and another', according to GV.
Connor's Court	Located on Tivoli Avenue.
Corrig Castle	It is now demolished but was located in Corrig Park.
Corrig Castle Terrace	Located in Northumberland Park.
Crimmin's Court	Not known.
Crofton Parade	Located in the area of Crofton Mews, Stable Lane, and Crofton Road.
Crofton Parade	Located on Lower George's Street.
Crofton Place	Not known, presumed off Crofton Road.
Cromer's Court	Located at the rear of No. 30 Kingstown Avenue. Edward Cromer is listed as lessor of all three dwellings. He is not listed as an occupier in any location in Ireland. No. 30 Kingstown Avenue was owned by 'Mat. Doyle and another'.
Cummin's Court	Located on Wellington Street.
Cunningham's Court	Located on Lower George's Street.
Darby's Court	The exact location is not known. Richard Darby lived in No. 1. He was lessor of four dwellings. George Darby was lessor of a further three dwellings.
Darcy's Court	Not known.
Delany's Court	According to GV, it was located 'off Ryder's Row'. It is listed alongside a number of courts in the vicinity of Lower George's Street. Joseph Delany was the listed lessor, but no person of that name is listed as living locally. Two locations called Ryder's Row can be found in Kingstown. One is located off York Street, later renamed York Road. It has twenty-eight cabins. There is also a Ryder's Row Lower on George's Street, according to the *Thom's* of 1852.
Diamond Place	Located on Patrick Street.
Dignam's Court (2)	Listed in *Thom's* of 1893 as being located between Nos 17 and 18 Mulgrave Street. This address is listed as Baylis Court, according to GV.
Dignan's Court AKA Dignams Court or Digmans Court	Located at the rear of 12 Rumley Avenue, now Mulgrave Street. The lessor was Lawrence Dignan, who lived at 12 Rumley Avenue.
Dixon's Cottages	Located in Sandycove.
Dockrell's Court	Not known.
Dolan's Court	Located in Mulgrave Street.

Address	Location
Dowling's Court	Located in Mulgrave Street.
Doyle's Court	Not known. William Doyle was the lessor for seven of these dwellings. Mrs Doyle was the occupier of No. 1.
Doyle's Lane	Not known.
Duff's Court	Located where the Carnegie Library now stands.
Duff's Court (2)	Not known.
Elden's Court and battery, East Pier	Not known. It must be close to East Pier.
Eldon's Court	Located in Mulgrave Street.
Eubank's Court	Located in Lower George's Street.
Eubank's Court (2)	Located at George's Place.
Evan's Court	Located at the rear of 11 Rumley Avenue. One dwelling was registered in the name of Murtagh Evans.
Fagan's Court	Located behind the premises now occupied by Just Beds in Lower George's Street.
Finnegan's Court	Located at the rear of Nos 96 to 99 Kingstown Avenue, now Patrick Street. Haliday reports that these dwellings share a privy and ashpit.
Finnegan's Court (2)	Located at rear of No. 15 Lower George's Street, with which it shared a privy and ashpit.
Fitzhenry's Court	Located at Paradise Row, now Patrick Street.
Fitzpatrick's Court	Located at Cross Avenue.
Flanagan's Court No. 1	Located at the rear of 8 Paradise Avenue. Mrs Flanagan was the listed lessor of the dwellings in the court, according to GV. She was the joint occupier of 8 Paradise Row, and was the lessor of seven dwellings on Paradise Avenue.
Flanagan's Court No. 2	Located at the rear of Nos 9 and 10 Paradise Avenue. Mrs Flanagan was listed as lessor of all but one of these dwellings.
Flynn's Court	Located at the rear of 28 Lower George's Street, according to GV. In 2015, No. 28 is an archway just two doors from O'Loughlins bar. However, the Ordnance Survey of Ireland (OSI) map of 1900 shows Flynn's Court a few doors away in a position which is now at the centre of the roadway at Library Road. Haliday lists it as sharing facilities with 24 Lower George's Street. Library Road was constructed in 1912.
Foley's Court	Located at the rear of 24 Kingstown Avenue, now Patrick Street, according to GV. Haliday lists it as being at 29 Kingstown Avenue. John Foley was the lessor of both 24 Kingstown Avenue and the dwellings behind it, but is not listed as the occupier of any property in Kingstown.
Foster's Court	Located on Patrick Street. James Foster lived in No. 4 and was the lessor of four of the dwellings.
Foster's Court (2)	Located on Cumberland Street.
Foster's Place	Located between Nos 10 and 11 Cumberland Street, according to Thom's.
Gannon's Row AKA Gannons Court	Located at Cross Avenue, according to Browne and at the rear of James' Place, according to GV. James Gannon is listed as the lessor of twenty properties in Kingstown and lived at number 37 Rumley Avenue, now Mulgrave Street.
Garvy's Court	Not known.
Goat Alley	Not known.
Goff's Court	Located at the rear of Nos 22 and 23 Cumberland Street.
Gough's Court	Not known.
Hall's Court	Located at the rear of 62 Kingstown Avenue, now Patrick Street. Mrs Hall was the lessor of these dwellings and lived at 62 Kingstown Avenue.
Hanlon's Court	Located on Mulgrave Street, according to Browne.
Hassard's Court AKA Echo Court AKA Acho Court	Rebuilt as Dominick Street. William Hassard was the lessor of all twenty-four dwellings, according to GV. The name Echo or Acho Court was associated with the nearby big house, Echo Lodge. William Hassard appears to have lived at Mountjoy Square in Dublin.
Healy's Court	Located at the rear of Nos 64 and 65 York Street, later renamed York Road. The lessor was Thomas Healy, who also held quite a few leases in Albert Place and Prospect Terrace as well as Nos 61 to 70 York Street (now York Road). There is no record of him living in Kingstown.
Hilton's Court	Located on Cumberland Street.
Hogan's Court	Not known.
Hope Court	Located on Patrick Street in the area of No. 96, according to the Ordnance Survey of Ireland in 1866.
Howard Place	Located between the Royal Marine Hotel and Gresham Terrace. The right-hand extension of the hotel is built over this site.
Hyne's Court	Located at the rear of Nos 28 and 29 Kingstown Avenue, now Patrick Street. John Hynes was the lessor and lived in No. 28 Kingstown Avenue.
Jenning's Court	Not known.
Jones's Court	Located at the rear of 9 Lower George's Street, now the location of a barber's shop called Champs. Mary Jones lived at 7 Lower George's Street.

Address	Location
Kelly's Court	Located on Patrick Street. The lessor of these twenty dwellings was John Kelly. John Kelly Senior lived at 6 Kelly's Court, while John Kelly Junior lived at No. 7, according to GV.
Kinsella's Court	Not known.
Knight's Cottages AKA Knights Court	Located on Kelly's Avenue.
Laceys Court, AKA Lacy's Court	Located on Mulgrave Street.
Larkin's Yard	Located on Turner's Avenue in the area of Cross Avenue.
Lerinimon's Court	Located on Patrick Street, according to Browne.
Long's Row	Located on Turner's Avenue in the area of Cross Avenue.
Lowry's Court	Located at the rear of No. 83 Kingstown Avenue, now Patrick Street. John Lowry was the lessor of one unit. John Lowry lived at 85 Kingstown Avenue.
Lyburn's Cottages	Not known.
Maher's Court	Located on Kingstown Avenue. The privy and ashpit are shared with nine houses from Nos 103 to 111, according to Haliday.
Marlow's Court AKA Marlow's Place	Located on Patrick Street, according to Browne. Matthew Marlow was the lessor for seven units and lived in No. 4.
Mar's Court or Mars Court	Located off Patrick Street between Nos 107 and 108, now Mike's Bikes and Gallagher Insurances. It now forms about half of the lane renamed in 2014 as Cantwell Lane, according to the Ordinance Survey of Ireland in 1866.
Martin's Court	Located on Patrick Street.
Matthew Terrace	Not known.
Mc Cormack's Court	Located at the rear of 70 Kingstown Avenue, now Patrick Street. William McCormack lived at 70 Kingstown Avenue.
McCormick's Court	Located on Clarence Street.
McEntee's Court	Not known.
McGillick Court	Located on Patrick Street.
Meledy's Court	Located at the rear of 2 Rumley Avenue, now Mulgrave Street. These were very low-valuation dwellings, according to GV. The lessor was Pierce Meledy, who owned the house at 2 Rumley Avenue and was also the lessor for Nos 3 and 4 Rumley Avenue.

Address	Location
Milliken's Court	Located at the junction of Paradise Row, now Convent Road, and Patrick Street. It was a narrow lane that has been widened at some time and has recently been renamed as Lynch Lane. There is no direct evidence of the origin of the name, but a Peter Milliken was the lessor of some houses on both Kingstown Avenue, now Patrick Street, and Paradise Row. Until about 1900, Paradise Row was a cul-de-sac and Milliken's Court was at the end of it.
Milliken's Court (2)	Not known. Haliday lists two places of this name, with six and eleven dwellings respectively.
Molloy's Court	Located between Nos 5 and 7 York Street, now York Road, according to Thom's of 1893.
Mooney's Court	Located on Patrick Street.
Moran's Court	Located on Patrick Street.
Mulgrave Place	Not known. It pre-dates the naming of Mulgrave Street.
Mullady's Court	Located at the rear of 33 Kingstown Avenue, now Patrick Street. The lessor was Pierce Mullady. He was possibly the same individual as Pierce Meledy, the owner and lessor associated with Meledy's Court.
Murphy's Court	Located at the rear of 75 Kingstown Avenue, now Patrick Street. John Murphy was the lessor and lived in 5 Murphy's Court.
Murphy's Lane	Not known.
Murray's Court	Located at the rear of 3 Rumley Avenue, now Mulgrave Street. James Murray was the lessor.
Murtagh's Court No. 1	Located at the rear of 15 Paradise Avenue, now Convent Row. The lessor was Murtagh Byrne who lived at 15 Paradise Avenue.
Murtagh's Court No. 2	Located at the rear of 17 Paradise Avenue, now Convent Row. The lessor was Murtagh Byrne who lived at 15 Paradise Avenue.
Needham's Court	Located at the rear of 78 and 79 Kingstown Avenue, now Patrick Street. James Needham was the lessor of these, and of 79 Kingstown Avenue. He lived at 80 Kingstown Avenue.
Nugents Court	Located on Mulgrave Street.
Nulty's Court	Located on Cumberland Street.
O'Brien's Court	Not known.
O'Carroll's Court No. 1	Located at the rear of 5 Rumley Avenue, now Mulgrave Street. Peter O'Carroll was the lessor of 5 Rumley Avenue and of the court dwellings. He was also the lessor of 6 Rumley Avenue, where the occupiers were 'Peter O'Carroll's Lodgers'. He lived at 7 Rumley Avenue.

Address	Location
O'Carroll's Court No. 2	Located at the rear of 6 Rumley Avenue.
Paradise Place	Not known.
Paradise Row (1849)	This address should not be confused with a later Paradise Row (below). This Paradise Row is listed in GV. The exact location is not known, but is believed to be in the area of Wolfe Tone Avenue.
Paradise Row	The section of Convent Road from Cross Avenue to the junction of the lane, now known as Lynch Lane. It was a cul-de-sac until about 1900, when two shops were demolished on Lower George's Street to create a through way from Paradise Row to Lower George's Street.
Pave Lane AKA Paved Lane	Located between Nos 13 and 14 Patrick Street. This lane ran through to Paradise Row, now Convent Road.
Penston's Court	Located on Mulgrave Street.
Pims Court	Located on Lower George's Street.
Reid's Court	Located on Patrick Street.
Roberts' Court or Robinsons Court	Located on Clarence Street.
Ryan's Court	Located between Nos 8 and 9 Mulgrave Street, according to the *Thom's* of 1893.
Sexton's Court (Clarence Street)	Located in the back gardens of the houses now located on Bentley Villas.
Sexton's Court (Lower George's Street)	Located on Lower George's Street.
Sexton's Court (Cumberland Street)	Located behind 26 Cumberland Street. About 1903 it was demolished and replaced by redbrick houses as part of the Kingstown Improvement Scheme.
Sexton's Court (York Street)	Located on York Street, now York Road.
Sharkey's Court	Located at the rear of 5 Wellington Place. Margaret Sharkey was the lessor of three of these dwellings, as well as of 5 Wellington Place.
Stable Lane	Likely to have been located between Upper George's Street and Gresham Terrace.
Stable Lane	Located at the rear of Crofton Terrace.
Stable Lane	Located off Northumberland Avenue.
Stephen's Court	Located at the rear of 76 Kingstown Avenue. Edward Stephens was the lessor and lived at 78 Kingstown Avenue.
Sword's Court	Located at the rear of 15 Kingstown Avenue. Michael Swords was the lessor and lived at 15 Kingstown Avenue.
Synnott Terrace	Not known.

Address	Location
Synnott's Court	Located on Cumberland Street. Listed as Sinnott's Court, according to Browne.
Synott's Court	Located on Patrick Street.
Tierney's Court	Located on Kelly's Avenue.
Tinch's Court	Located at the rear of 5 Tivoli Avenue. George Tinch was the lessor and lived at 4 Tivoli Avenue.
Tivoli Avenue	Located in the laneway to the rear of the houses on the west side of Desmond Avenue, according to DLBHS.
Toole's Court	Located on Patrick Street, according to Browne, or Cross Avenue, according to Haliday.
Toole's Court (2)	Located on Paradise Row.
Toomey's Court	Located on Wellington Street.
Tully's Row	Located in the area of the early village of Dunlary. It consisted of a row of about ten small houses which were demolished in the late 1850s to make room for the road in front of Nos 20 to 28 Longford Terrace, Monkstown. It is shown in Ordnance Survey maps between 1837 and 1860.
Turner's Avenue	Located off Cross Avenue.
Turner's Lane or Paradise Place	Located off Cross Avenue.
Valetta Avenue	Not known. It was either on York Road or Lower George's Street.
Walch's Court	Located at the rear of Nos 19 and 20 Mulgrave Street, with which they shared a privy and ashpit.
Walnut's Court	Located close to where O'Loughlin's pub now stands. Joseph Walnut lived at 27 Lower George's Street, and this court was at the rear of his house.
Wellington Place	Located off George's Place.
White's Court	Located on Clarence Street.
White's Court (1)	Located at the rear of 7 Paradise Avenue, which shows the names of 'Thomas White and Lodgers' as occupiers. The lessor of 7 Paradise Avenue was Revd Bartholomew Sheridan, parish priest of Kingstown Roman Catholic parish. Thomas White was the lessor of the houses in White's Court.
White's Court (2)	Located on Patrick Street. Browne and Haliday each list two separate courts by this name.
William's Court AKA Williams Cottages	Located on George's Place.

A Family of
'Invisible Kingstown'

The year 1816 was a very important year in the history of the town, then named Dunleary. It was the year in which the government committed to the construction of the harbour and passed the necessary enabling legislation. It was also the year in which Henry Connor was born. Henry spent his adult life hauling coal in the quays and coalyards. He married Eliza Donnelly and was 44 when his daughter, Mary, was born. She was 16 when Henry contracted typhoid fever and died at the newly built St Michael's Hospital in 1876 aged 60.

Two years later, when Mary was 18, she married Patrick McLoughlin. At that time she was listed as living at 37 Cumberland Street, Kingstown, but this address is probably a clerical error as No. 37 never existed. Soon thereafter, they were living at 3 Cumberland Street. In the 1901 census, the house is listed as having four rooms, with just one window in front, and is classified as third class.

Mary's husband, Patrick, was an Arklow-born seafarer. At the time of the marriage, he was listed as a 40-year-old crewmember on board the *William Thomas*, a collier. Records show that a shipbuilding company called William Thomas & Sons of Anglesea in Wales had located a number of vessels at Arklow about this time.

At some time, Mary and Patrick dropped the prefix 'Mc' from the family name, and became the Loughlins.

Children came in quick succession. Infant mortality was high in those days, but all of Patrick and Mary's children survived. Over the next thirteen years, John, Henry, Patrick, Miles, William, Michael, and Laurence were born, and for almost each one of these births the records show a change in the address of the family. Like many of the poor in Kingstown, they had no fixity of tenure – if they could not pay the rent, they had to move. They had addresses at:

1 3 Cumberland Street
2 Albert Terrace (a row of four small houses on Crofton Road which are still standing)
3 Seaview House (there were a number of houses of this name in the area)
4 3 Cumberland Street (again)
5 Albert Place (this was demolished and replaced by Smyth's Gardens)
6 24 Cumberland Street – this house had six rooms. Many of the houses on Cumberland Street were tenements, occupied by more than one family

Mary was widowed when her husband, Patrick, died in 1891 aged fifty-three. The youngest child, Laurence was just four months old. The eldest was not yet thirteen.

Laurence was just a year old when this photo of the family (minus one of Mary's sons) was taken in 1892. All of them are dressed in their best clothes.

About the time of the 1901 census, the family was photographed again, and this time all were present. By this stage Mary had bought a sewing machine and was eking out a living as a dressmaker. The stylish dress she is wearing is almost certainly of her own making. Henry is clearly employed at sea and proudly displays the name of his ship, the *Munster*. John is also a seafarer, and the younger boys are at school.

At the time of the 1901 census, Mary was recorded as living at Connor's Court, a small court of four dwellings. There were two places called Connor's Court, both of them having four dwellings, and it is unclear in which one the Loughlin family lived. One place called Connor's Court was at the rear of 15 Rumley Avenue (Musgrave Street), while the other was on Tivoli Avenue (demolished about 1903 and partly replaced by Desmond Avenue).

John, the eldest, was not recorded in the 1901 census; he was probably at sea. Henry, 18, was a cook on the mail boat while Miles, 15, was listed as a 'Gas Meter Carrier'. William, aged 13, is already working as a messenger-boy. The other boys are at school.

Under the Kingstown Improvement Scheme, Mary was able to obtain a new house at 48 Paradise Row (Convent Road) about 1905. It was a modest house, listed as having three rooms, and as having four windows in front. It was the best house she had in her life. In 1911 she was living there with Henry, William, Michael and Laurence. She was still dressmaking. Henry had become a chief cook on the mail boat. William and Michael were listed as labourers, while Laurence was listed as a messenger.

Mary Loughlin died at 48 Paradise Row on 28 December 1913 aged 53, and was interred at Deansgrange Cemetery (plot F/33/W).

We are grateful to Frances Fletcher, great-granddaughter of Mary Loughlin, for the above information and photos.

HOUSING IN KINGSTOWN IN 1849

OVERVIEW

A casual visitor to Kingstown in 1849 would likely have reported that it was a very pleasant place with rows of fine houses, grouped around pleasant parks, with excellent services and shops. Poverty was largely hidden from view.

An analysis of Griffith's Valuation from 1849 shows the extent to which poverty was hidden in the backyards of houses and shops on the main streets, or in cul-de-sacs which would not be seen except by those who searched them out. Our analysis of Griffith shows that 40 per cent of the dwellings of the town were tiny, poor-quality 'cabins', and this figure understates the number of situations where the poor lived in cramped or otherwise unsatisfactory conditions.

GRIFFITH'S VALUATION

Over the period from the 1830s through to the 1860s, a comprehensive survey was undertaken throughout Ireland to assess and value all land and buildings and to create a baseline for levying local taxes. The survey results for Kingstown were printed in 1849, while the Great Famine was still in progress.

The Griffith's Valuation books provide a full list of the dwellings on each street, road, court, or lane, with the name of the occupier, and the assessed valuation. Most dwellings were built on leasehold land and the name of the immediate lessor (landlord) is also shown.
The assessed valuation is based upon the annual rent which the property might produce.

VALUATION THRESHOLDS

In the earlier valuations conducted by Griffith's team, only those properties with a valuation in excess of £3 were surveyed, thereby reducing the workload of surveying, but eliminating the houses of the very poor. It was then discovered that this did not eliminate a sufficient number, and a higher threshold of £5 was then used.

These thresholds are significant. The fact that there were not many below the £3 threshold indicates that this threshold would apply only to the very poor housing of those in extreme poverty. The fact that surveying houses with a valuation below £5 was not considered worthwhile indicates that the government thought they would produce little by way of local tax.

It must be made clear that Griffith had switched to a policy of comprehensive valuation of all properties before he started on the valuation of Kingstown, and so every mansion, house, cottage, and cabin in Kingstown is included in the Griffith's Valuation lists.

For the purpose of our analysis of housing in Kingstown, we have taken Griffith's Valuation and applied the £3 and £5 thresholds. We have not found it possible to indicate precisely the type of dwelling that would have met these thresholds in Kingstown, but we can indicate that:

1   A £3 valuation would likely indicate a small one-room dwelling with no water or sewerage. It might have a mud floor, an insubstantial roof, door, and window.

2 A £5 might have had a larger space, possibly two small rooms or a more substantial roof, doors and windows. It also had no water or sewerage.

Our analysis of Griffith's Valuation covered the area from Old Dunleary to the People's Park and from the seafront inland to include Corrig Road, Tivoli Road, York Road, and Lower Glenageary Road. It therefore covers the town and the immediately surrounding area. We have attempted to eliminate from our analysis any building that is clearly not a habitation. However, in those days, almost all shops and many other business premises appear to have had some living accommodation, and are included by us as dwellings.

Our analysis of Griffith's Valuation of Kingstown covered 1,381 dwellings.

Griffith's Valuation 1849, Kingstown	Number of Dwellings	Per cent of total
Dwellings with valuations below £3	281	20.3%
Dwellings with valuations between £3 and £5	269	19.5%
Subtotal	550	39.8%
Other dwellings	831	60.2%
Total	1,381	100.0%

The above analysis almost certainly understates the accommodation problem for the poor of Kingstown.

1 A tenement house with multi-occupancy would be recorded as a single holding with a substantial valuation, even though each family there might have only a single room.

2 Families of lowly paid shop employees invariably lived over the shop in cramped accommodation, which is included in the valuation of the shop.

LOCATIONS OF POVERTY

In the Kingstown of 1849, there were, of course, certain ghetto areas where all of the dwellings were of poor quality. Examples included Hassard's Court, Tivoli Avenue, and Paradise Avenue, each comprising over twenty dwellings, all of which were demolished many years ago. These three locations were within a stone's throw of each other and surrounded by a number of smaller courts and streets where most or all housing was of poor quality, indicating extreme poverty. These areas are now the locations of Convent Road, Cross Avenue, Mill's Street, Dominick Street, Wolfe Tone Avenue, Desmond Avenue, and Tivoli Terrace East.

There were certain areas of mixed housing where the poor and the more fortunate citizens often lived in close proximity to one another on the same street. Examples can be seen in Kingstown Avenue, now Patrick Street, and Cumberland Street. In both of these areas, many houses and former shops, which pre-date Griffith, still survive, but the low-quality housing has long since disappeared.

The street courts were an important element of the mixed housing. Along the main streets, wherever there was an alleyway, this was almost invariably filled with small dwellings to form a court, which was given a family surname, such as Flynn's Court, Murphy's Court, and so on. 'Cabins' was the term frequently used by *Thom's Directory* and a number of other sources to describe these dwellings.

One of the best examples of courts on the main street is the area where Library Road meets Lower George's Street, and the adjacent site where the Carnegie Library building now stands, recently vacated. Both the road and the library date from about 1912. This area had three courts, Duff's Court, Flynn's Court and Ball's Court, all based around short narrow alleyways.

There is an unnamed laneway that today runs parallel to and between Patrick Street and Mulgrave Street, providing access to backyards of houses 86–107 Patrick Street and 1–22 Mulgrave Street. In 1849 many of those backyards were small but densely packed courts. These included, on the Mulgrave Street side alone, Baylis Court, also listed as Dignam's Court, and a second Dignam's, or Dignan's Court, Connor's Court, Meledy's Court, Murray's Court, two separate courts called O'Carroll's Court, Ryan's Court, Walch's Court, as well as a number of others whose precise location on the street cannot be placed.

OWNERSHIP AND LEASEHOLDING

Much of the land on which Kingstown/Dún Laoghaire was built had been acquired by the Lords Longford and de Vesci around 1799, and had been leased under ninety-nine-year leases from 1804. Together these lords were known locally as the 'Lords of the Soil' and that appellative is frequently used in the records of meetings of the local authorities over the years.

Griffith's Valuation lists the name of the 'immediate lessor' for each property. For properties where rent is paid directly to a landlord, this listing shows the name of the landlord. However, in nineteenth-century Kingstown, subleases at various levels were commonplace. The person shown as the immediate lessor may be a middleman or an agent on behalf of a landlord. Where a landlord holds a large estate, one would expect to see his name frequently appearing, or alternatively, he would likely have a small number of agents whose names would appear frequently. Although the Longford and de Vesci estates held sway in Kingstown, this does not show in the valuation records.

In a letter to the *Irish Independent* newspaper on 6 June 1905, Messrs J.R. Stewart and sons, on behalf of the Lords Longford and de Vesci, stated, 'That there are many poor houses in Kingstown no one will dispute, but the members of the Urban District Council are well aware that the houses were built during the term of the old leases, when the present owners had unfortunately, no powers of interference; and it is a remarkable fact that during the time they were owned by middlemen – some of them members of former Councils.' The 'old leases' were those in force from about 1804–1903.

In examining the immediate lessors in Kingstown, it appears that leases are very widely dispersed. There is no indication of dominant lessors. There were a couple of people who held large portfolios of leases within a given street. Among those few were Thomas Gresham, who was the immediate lessor for all of the very fine houses and hotels on Gresham Terrace, now demolished, and Thomas Tilley who held leases for eight houses on Haddington Terrace.

Among the courts and lanes, the person listed as the immediate lessor can be identified easily in many cases and tends to live locally. The lessors mainly fall into three categories:

- Situations where a court has been established in the backyard of a main-street house or shop.
    - In many of these situations, the immediate lessor is the occupier of the main-street house.
    - In a small number of cases, he is the occupier of a nearby main-street house. In these cases, it is likely that the lessor gets a rent from each tenant. In most cases, the court may be named with the surname of that lessor.

- Situations where the immediate lessor is a resident within the court. In some cases, this person occupies the most valuable dwelling within the court, but this is not always true. In these cases, it is most likely that the named lessor is acting in the role of agent on behalf of a landlord. In some cases of this type, the court is named after him.

- Situations where the lessor cannot be identified locally. An example is William Hassard who is the immediate lessor of all twenty-four dwellings in Hassard's Court, now Dominick Street. Four people of that name show up on Griffith's Valuation, and the most likely one is William Hassard of Mountjoy Street, Dublin.

FURTHER RESEARCH

There is a need for further research to establish and document the actual ownership of these properties.

HALIDAY'S SANITATION SURVEY, 1866

One of the last acts of Charles Haliday (1789–1866) before he died was the preparation of a letter to the Kingstown Town Commissioners describing the conditions of the poor in Kingstown, with particular reference to sanitation. The letter was published posthumously by his friend and biographer, Dr Thomas More Madden.

Haliday was a highly respected historian, businessman, and campaigner seeking to improve the conditions of the poor and reduce the incidence of disease. He lived at Monkstown Park, now the location of Monkstown Christian Brothers' College.

The Haliday letter, published in 1867 by Madden as *A Statistical Inquiry into the Sanitary Condition of Kingstown*, describes in words and tables the conditions in over 140 courts in which, according to his estimate, one-third of the population lived.

To put this letter in context, it is necessary to be aware of the nature of sanitation in 1866. The flush toilet had only been in mass production in Britain for about ten years. Installed water closets (WCs) would have been very rare in Ireland, even in the homes of the wealthy. The water supply to Kingstown, sourced from the Vartry river at Roundwood, was not yet flowing and the earlier local water systems were limited. The Vartry water supply commenced in 1871. Maps of the time show wells and pumps in a number of areas. The wealthier folk would likely have had a dry toilet or privy at the end of the garden and chamber pots for use during the night.

Haliday's report described the situations in individual courts. In McCormick's Court on Clarence Street, there were 100 inhabitants in 24 houses and cottages with earthen floors. There was no source of water. There were one privy and one ashpit for the entire court. The Town Commissioners employed four men with carts to remove the human excrement from places like this and to dispose of it in a facility in the Rochestown area.

Take the case of Codd's Court:

opening into George's Street, and open to the view of every person passing through that street. This court, which is not quite eight feet wide, contains five houses and three cottages without any rear whatsoever. It is without pavement or flagging, without sewer or drain, without water or gas, without privy or ash-pit, and, like some of the other dwelling places of the labouring classes in Kingstown, it is without any receptacle for filth and offal except the centre of the court, into which all is cast after nightfall, having been retained within doors during the day, tainting the athmosphere [*sic*] of those wretched apartments, in which, as in almost all other cases, whole families eat, drink, and sleep. Nor is it easy to prevent this filth from accumulating, the court being so narrow that scavengers can only use a hand-cart in their efforts to cleanse it. It is but just, however, to the owner of the cottages to add, that after a delay of many years, he says that he is now about to build a privy and ash-pit for the three cottages; but the five houses and their unfortunate inmates are to remain in their present condition.

In his report, Haliday located and recorded 644 'deficient' dwellings in which he surveyed the sanitary arrangements. He does not clearly define 'deficient', but from the context of his letter, we can deduce that he is talking about the size of the dwellings, the lack of basic facilities, the cold and dampness. He links the survey with the prevalence of disease. Indeed the letter was written during a cholera epidemic in which 124 people died in Kingstown in a period of ten weeks in 1866.

Haliday makes an interesting point. In his view, most of the wealthier citizens are unaware of the existence of the courts and of the conditions within them. This may be partly explained by the fact that the dwellings of the poor are almost invariably located in cul-de-sacs into which the wealthier folk may have no reason to enter.

He goes on:

I solicit your attention – for the fact that in a place like Kingstown, such courts and lanes exist, and have long existed, apparently unnoticed? Here we have a comparatively small town – a town which may be walked over from one end to the other within an hour – a fashionable watering-place – the Summer resort of invalids seeking health, and the permanent residence of some of the wealthy citizens of Dublin; and yet in connection with the principal street and almost in the centre of the town, we find upwards of one hundred courts and lanes in an abominable state of filth and neglect, mostly unpaved – without sewers or drains – without privies or ash-pits – without any water supply – without even a pump – and being without gas lamps or other lights, they are at night involved in darkness, and become the receptacles for filth of all kinds; and yet, as they contain nearly eight hundred houses or cottages, inhabited by four thousand or five thousand human beings, they are the dwelling houses of one third of the entire population of Kingstown.

A couple of examples from Haliday may illustrate the severity of the problem:

- Albert Place, off York Road, had twenty-four dwellings with one shared privy and one ashpit. In these twenty-four dwellings, we may speculate that the population might have been more than 100.
- Baymount Court, which was entered through an archway on Cumberland Street, at the location of the Dún Laoghaire Institute of Further Education had twenty dwellings. It did not have even a single privy. It only had one ashpit.

Fuller details of Haliday's survey are shown in the Appendix.

Haliday himself died of cholera before he managed to complete the letter to accompany the survey.

The Haliday report was published in early 1867 and was the subject of newspaper editorials at the time, but little else. With a sense of frustration, Madden wrote to the *Freeman's Journal* on 19 June, complaining that nothing was being done to improve the situation. He stated that a Mr McEvoy, the honourable secretary of the committee of ratepayers of Kingstown, had written to confirm the literal accuracy of Haliday's findings.

Madden was a widely travelled person who had detailed knowledge of conditions around the world. He had studied in Dublin, France, and Spain, and had recently returned from North Africa and Australia. He was shortly to take up a position at the Rotunda Hospital. He said in his letter:

The sewerage of the poorer parts of Kingstown is still worse than that of any civilised town I have ever visited; and I believe that I am as conversant with the medical topography and sanitary arrangements of foreign countries as any person in this city. Before I edited Mr Haliday's – 'Letter to the Town Commissioners of Kingstown', I carefully examined nearly all the lanes and courts of the township, and the state of things which presented itself, familiar as I was with scenes of poverty and misery, was positively appalling.

In the majority of the houses, courts, and lanes inhabited by the poor of Kingstown, sewerage is utterly neglected, public decency is outraged, and the public health injured, by the deficiency of latrines and sewers, by the accumulation of filth in the houses and their vicinity, and by the pestilential effluvia thus generated. In some of these lanes there is no latrine whatever; in others there is one place of accommodation common to six or eight houses. It is obvious that the spread of any epidemic, and most especially of one like cholera, must be increased by a large number of persons, sick as well as healthy, being obliged to resort to the same latrine.

In fairness, it must be said that both Haliday and Madden appear to have been unreasonable in their demands, and that this might have contributed to their failure to achieve major change. The demand that 'No house, however small, should be allowed to remain without a properly constructed water-closet, well equipped with water' would likely have been considered by the Town Commissioners as too far beyond realistic, given the overall state of the water and sewerage infrastructure at the time. He went further to say that 'All landlords in Kingstown should be obliged to construct one of these essentials to health and decency in every house they own'. Madden went further to demand that there should be a minimum amount of space per person, and some of the figures quoted might be considered high even by twenty-first-century standards.

Ten years later, in an inquiry held in the town, the Haliday report was widely quoted by the presiding QC. He demanded progress reports. There was much conflict in the evidence given and the conclusion was that some work had been done, but there was still a lot to do.

TAXATION INQUIRY, 1877

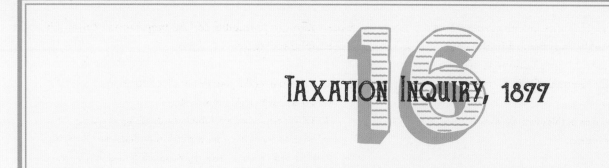

The period from 1867 to 1877 saw great improvements in urban life, and these would have been quite evident to a visitor to the town. The public water system, sourced from the river Vartry, through the Stillorgan Reservoir, which came available in the preceding decade, had resulted in a major improvement throughout the town. It provided pure water for drinking and enabled the proper installation of water closets in the better houses. For the poorer classes, a public tap in each area reduced the need for drawing water from a distance and ensured that the water was drinkable. The presence of clean water would have helped to reduce the incidence of disease and the risk of epidemic. It would also have reduced the foul smells as the water was used to 'scour and wash out the lanes'.

There were improvements to the town's sewerage system, but major questions had arisen in relation to the implementation of those sewers, and in relation to their efficiency. The public lighting system had improved. Some work had been done to demolish a few of the worst houses of the poor, but no schemes had been proposed to rehouse the displaced.

In summary, there were improvements that benefited everyone, but the relative differential between rich and poor was as wide as ever.

In 1877, an inquiry was undertaken by the Taxation of Towns Inquiry Commission into affairs at Kingstown. Much of the evidence given was concerned with water, sanitation, and sewage. Similar inquiries were undertaken in fifty-six towns and cities across Ireland.

The Commission spent nine days between 5 April and 29 June taking evidence in Kingstown from over thirty witnesses. The witnesses included employees of the Town Commissioners, elected commissioners, local medical experts, and other interested parties. Over 100 pages of evidence were documented in relation to Kingstown. The final report treated Kingstown and Dalkey as exceptional among towns and cities. They were published as a separate supplement, with a comment that this took longer in evidence-gathering than did the whole of the rest of Dublin.

In its conclusions, the inquiry referred back to the Haliday survey of 1866/7 and reported that:

The sanitary condition of the township is far from satisfactory … In the year 1866, the sanitary condition of Kingstown was very bad, as will appear from a report by Mr Charles Haliday … with notes in the year 1867 by Dr Thomas More Madden … It will be seen from the evidence of Dr O'Flaherty, the sanitary officer, that much has been done to improve the condition of the places referred to by Mr Haliday, but that there is still a great deal that has not been done, and he also stated that he could show us courts 'that ought to be swept off the face of the earth,' and further that if an epidemic were now to break out in Kingstown, it would probably be attended with serious consequences. Mr Doyle likewise stated that there were some exceedingly poor houses in the centre of Kingstown … the whole of these places should be levelled to the ground.

The inquiry was conducted by William A. Exham, Queen's Counsel (QC) and Mr E.B. Lawless, QC. Both were highly experienced in the conduct of inquiries. They recorded the responses to 3,266 questions in their book of evidence. Together they questioned Dr Jeremiah O'Flaherty:

LAWLESS: Are you one of the sanitary officers of this town, doctor?

O'FLAHERTY: Yes, since the act came into operation.

LAWLESS: You know Kingstown well?

O'FLAHERTY: Yes, I knew the town for many years prior to the passing of the Sanitary Act.

LAWLESS: Have you lived there for a considerable time?

O'FLAHERTY: Yes, since the year 1855.

LAWLESS: What is the sanitary condition of the houses of the poorer classes in Kingstown?

O'FLAHERTY: The sanitary accommodation is defective by reason of the structures.

LAWLESS: Do you mean to say that the structures or houses are not sufficiently large to afford the accommodation required?

O'FLAHERTY: Yes, because the accommodation for the poor consists generally of cabins and ground floors, and when the weather is bad the ground floors are mud floors.

LAWLESS: Are these old or recently constructed houses that you speak of?

O'FLAHERTY: I think they are old – yes old. I believe that I know all of the old houses of the town.

Some discussion about responsibility for the preparation of monthly and quarterly reports followed, then:

LAWLESS: Are the houses of the poor people here sufficiently looked after with regard to cleanliness?

O'FLAHERTY: No, I don't think they are. I think the dwellings of the poor very defective. Many of them are without yards, and have merely mud floors, so that in wet weather the floors are turned into a state of mud, and perhaps two or three pigs, a goat, and a donkey are kept.

LAWLESS: In the houses?

O'FLAHERTY: No, not in the houses, but in the yards.

LAWLESS: In those cases in which pigs or other animals are kept are they kept close to the dwellings?

O'FLAHERTY: Yes, they are immediately outside the back door.

LAWLESS: Is that so close as to be injurious to health?

O'FLAHERTY: Yes, I think so.

LAWLESS: When a state like that exists, is it looked after by the sanitary officers sufficiently?

O'FLAHERTY: Yes, so far as I can see, I think they look after it.

EXHAM: (to O'Flaherty) Why don't they get rid of the animals altogether, at least why don't they remove them from dangerous proximity to the dwellings of the people?

O'FLAHERTY: That is not for me to say.

EXHAM: Is the proximity dangerous?

O'FLAHERTY: That is my opinion.

Exham introduced a copy of Haliday's survey of 1866/7 and quoted a passage:

EXHAM: 'In the majority of the houses, courts, and lanes inhabited by the poor of Kingstown, sewerage is utterly neglected, public decency is outraged, and the public health is injured by the deficiency of latrines and sewers, by the accumulation of filth in the houses and their vicinity, and by the pestilential effluvia thus generated.' Is that true, Dr O'Flaherty?

O'FLAHERTY: Yes, I believe it was quite true at the time the report was made, but it is not so now.

EXHAM: Is it not true in any respect now? If not, tell us what has been done since?

O'FLAHERTY: All the places to which that report refers are now provided with proper drainage.

EXHAM: Efficient drainage?

O'FLAHERTY: They are provided with surface drainage.

EXHAM: All the places referred to?

O'FLAHERTY: The majority of them.

EXHAM: Are the majority of these places provided with proper latrines or privies?

O'FLAHERTY: They are and the better parts of the town have been sewered since the publication of Mr Haliday's report.

EXHAM: Will the poor people get the benefit of the sewerage?

O'FLAHERTY: Well, not as much as persons residing in the better parts of the town and in the outlying districts.

EXHAM: Is the general condition of the poorer parts of the town better now than when it was described by Mr Haliday in this report?

O'FLAHERTY: I think it is and the introduction of the Vartry water has made a great improvement in the condition of the poorer residents of Kingstown. Before its introduction the poor people were obliged to use great economy in their use of water. They had to make a bucket of water do a great deal, and they had to have it delivered to them at their doors by means of a donkey. Now, they have good water in abundance – I must say in their very doors.

As the interrogators read more passages from Haliday's report, O'Flaherty and other witnesses confirmed that:

- McCormick's Court had been demolished.
- Gough's Court had been demolished.
- Baymount Court had been partly demolished but the sewerage in the remaining part was very defective.
- Cod's Court had been sewered, watered, and lighted in the past few years and there was one privy there.
- Albert Court was a large area in which the dwellings were built against the walls. They had no back doors, only front doors.

There was an interesting interchange at the end of the session. Lawless asked if the Town Commissioners had taken any notice of Haliday's 1867 report.

Myles Kelly, town commissioner: I never heard of it before.
Town Clerk: In 1869, I heard of this letter.
Mr Pallas, a civil engineer: We had it in 1867 when I was engineer to the board.

It is surprising that Myles Kelly (1816-1883) had not heard of Haliday's report. He had been active in liberal and Catholic causes in the town from an early age. He lived at 1 Albert Terrace, just three doors from his pub, the Yacht Tavern. The Yacht Tavern premises is now occupied by Scrumdiddly's Ice Cream. Kelly was a town commissioner for more than thirty years, and was highly influential in the project to develop St Michael's Hospital, where he was chairman of the board on two occasions. He was one of the very few Catholics to become a member of the Poor Law Guardians of Rathdown Workhouse.

IN SUMMARY

It would appear that some progress was made towards alleviating the plight of the poor of the area, but this was mainly due to developments such as the availability of water, rather than through any pressure from public opinion or from campaigners such as Haliday. Later reports suggest that little progress was made in the subsequent twenty years.

THE BROWNE REPORT, 1900 (PUBLISHED 1902)

In the year 1900, Dr T.J. Browne, medical inspector, undertook a survey of housing and sanitation in the poorer areas of Kingstown. Similar reports were prepared on most towns in Ireland at the time by Browne and others. He was therefore experienced in such matters. His analysis of Kingstown is far more extensive than that of any other town he examined, and his comments are more damning. 'Report on the Sanitary Circumstances and Administration of the Kingstown Urban District' by Dr T. J. Browne', was published 1902. It is a section of a much larger report; 'Supplement to the Twenty-Ninth Annual Report of The Local Government Board for Ireland 1900–1' subtitled 'Reports on the Sanitary Circumstances and Administration of cities and towns in Ireland, and of the Precautionary Measures respecting Plague taken by local authorities at the various ports'.

Browne did not mince his words. According to him, 'One third of the entire population may be classified as poor'. He identified 1,007 houses of the poorer class in 121 courts and laneways and attached details to his report. Browne included Sandycove and Glasthule within Kingstown.

A considerable proportion are barely fit for habitation and many are quite unfit. In many instances, there are no back-yards to the houses and they are built back to back in close confined courts, shut out from sunlight and air. The worst of these courts are to be found off Patrick Street, George's Street, Clarence Street, Cumberland Street, Cross Avenue, Paradise Street, Turner's Avenue, and Callaghan's Lane.

His list therefore includes almost all of the main thoroughfares of the town except Marine Road.

Additionally, he identified 355 tenement houses where families occupied a single room in many cases. With regard to these houses, he said they were 'of the worst description and fit for nothing except demolition'.

Browne stated that the population was estimated at 16,491. According to him states that about one-third, approximately 5,500, of the population was poor. Given the typical family size in that period it seems reasonable to assume at least four people per house living in the houses of the poor, and more than ten people living in each tenement house. If, however, we apply those factors to Browne's figures of 1,007 houses and 355 tenement houses of the poor, the result is more than 7,500, suggesting that Browne underestimated the overall poverty figure by a considerable amount.

The 1901 census, taken after Browne's survey but published before Browne's report, found Browne's estimate of 16,491 to be a slight underestimate but this did not explain the difference.

CHANGES IN URBAN LIFE AND ADMINISTRATION

Over the thirty years preceding the Browne report, there had been very considerable changes in the nature of urban living in Ireland and Britain. These were things which we now take for granted. Browne describes how many of these changes further widened the gap between rich and poor:

Paved streets	In 1870, there were few if any paved streets in Kingstown. By 1900, the main streets had been paved.
Clean water	In 1870, there was no public water system. All water was sourced from private wells and pumps. By 1900, all the houses of the wealthier classes had running water. The poorer classes had at least access to a tap or fountain nearby.
Sewerage	By 1900, all houses in Kingstown with a value of £12 or greater were connected to the sewage system. 'Those of a smaller valuation have no house drains, but have gully-traps in the yards, or in some convenient place for the reception of house slops.'
Flush toilets	Most wealthier and middle-income house owners had installed WCs by 1900. The Browne report shows that 'in some of the poorer localities, privy middens constitute the means of disposal [of excrement]. As a rule, one privy serves for several houses. The privies are connected with ashpits, and are, for the most part, kept in a foul and filthy state. Their construction is defective, and soakage into the surrounding soil takes place.'
Household refuse	There was no regular public system for removal of refuse in 1870. It was introduced in Kingstown in 1896. The death rate from contagious diseases was almost immediately halved. By 1900, there were twenty-four men with eight horses and carts undertaking domestic scavenging and transporting refuse to a landfill site in a disused brickfield at Rochestown. Browne considered that the site, which included a manure depot, was objectionable.
Public lighting	In 1870, gas lighting had only recently been introduced to Kingstown. By 1900, 450 gaslights were operating.

TENEMENTS

During the Victorian period, the understanding of the word 'tenement' changed, and care must be taken in relation to documents using the term. In Griffith's Valuation, the word is used to mean any property occupied by a tenant. In 1849, virtually all houses in Kingstown were listed as tenements. By the end of the century, the word had come to mean a house occupied by two or more separate families. Browne uses the term in relation to groups of houses in which each house was occupied by more than two families, and probably by one family in each room or pair of rooms.

The tenements of Kingstown were different from those of Dublin. The infamous tenements of Dublin were, in many cases, large Georgian four-storey houses pre-dating the 1801 Act of Union. The tenements of Kingstown were both smaller and newer. With the exception of Cumberland Street, Clarence Street, York Road, and the first few houses of Lower George's Street, there were no houses over 100 years old. Browne describes the tenements as being 'of the worst description, and fit for nothing except demolition'. The most plausible explanation is that houses were hastily built to very poor standards during the very rapid expansion of Kingstown between 1820 and 1840. In terms of size, they were typically modest two-storey houses.

In his survey, Browne identified the lavatory arrangements in each house, whether water-based or otherwise, and classified the various types of dry-toilet arrangements.

Browne's survey identified 355 tenement houses, of which about 260 were in the town or close to the town. He did not attempt to identify the number of families who occupied these houses, but from his description, it is safe to assume that the average number of families in each house was almost certainly more than three. This means that 800 or more families were living in these tenements:

Street/road	Number of tenements	Sanitary arrangements			
		Number with WC	Number with privy	Number with ashpit	Number with bin
Patrick Street	35	35			35
Mulgrave Street	35	35			35
Paradise Row	9		2	1	
Cross Avenue	14	14			14
Tivoli Avenue	22		4	4	
Turner's Avenue	15		4	4	
Lower George's Street	8	8			8
Clarence Street	8	8			8
Cumberland Street	11	11			11
Dunleary	5	5			5
York Street	10	10			10
Kelly's Avenue	6	6			6
George's Place	10	10			10
Lower Mountown	6		6	6	
Monkstown Avenue	11	11			11
Glenageary Road	13		9	9	
Upper George's Street	10	10			10
Glasthule	28	28		10	
Eden Road	4		3	3	

These dwellings are generally overcrowded, and are not kept clean or in a good state of repair. A family occupies each room, the rooms being small and deficient in ventilation and lighting. In fact, the slum property in Kingstown is of the worst description, and fit for nothing except demolition. The question of the housing of the working classes in Kingstown Urban District is one which must sooner or later engage the attention of the Sanitary Authority. The leases of most of this class of property will expire in two or three years, when, in all probability, the houses, or a large number of them, will be demolished. The sooner, therefore, the better the question of providing dwellings for the working classes is considered.

The leases identified by Browne as being due to expire were those created as ninety-nine-year leases commencing about 1804 and owned by the Longford, de Vesci, and Carysfort estates. The lease related to the land, regardless of the date when the house was built on it.

A detailed examination of the 1901 census sheds more light on tenement houses and supports Browne's thesis. It shows seven tenement houses in Clarence Street with 118 occupants or 17 people per tenement. If the pattern of the Clarence Street tenements were repeated throughout the 260 tenement houses, then about 4,500 of the poorer classes lived in tenements.

Clarence Street in the 1901 census								
House number	1	2	3	5	7	8	9	Totals
Number of distinct families	5	4	2	5	4	4	6	30
Total number of occupants	15	15	8	22	18	16	24	118
Total number of rooms	6	7	7	3 (?)	7	5	6	

Note: house No. 1 also has a coal office occupying at least one room; houses 4 and 6 are not tenements; the return for house No. 5 is clearly incorrect in showing it as having three rooms.

Browne identified 260 houses as tenements, dispersed as in the table below.

RECOMMENDATIONS

Browne was the master of concise and direct language in issuing his recommendations, which were as follows:

- The clearance of the worst slum areas and the provision of healthy dwellings for the working classes.
- The abolition of the midden privy system and the substitution of the water-carriage or pail systems. He recommended the provision of separate closet accommodation, as, where closets are used in common by several families, they are invariably kept in a filthy state.
- The registration and inspection of common lodging houses. He also recommended the strict enforcement of housing bye-laws.
- The repair of sewers, where defective.
- The strict enforcement of the regulations respecting dairies, cow sheds, and milk shops.

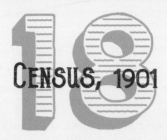

CENSUS, 1901

The 1901 census set out to record details of everyone who was present in Ireland on the night of 31 March 1901. It recorded their personal details and details of the buildings they occupied. Certain issues arise in relation to that census:

- Some entire addresses from the poorer areas of the town appear to have been omitted. This is a local issue and related to the administration of the census.
- The census purported to classify the housing stock in each area, using a points system of grading for each house. The classification system was hopelessly inadequate and is meaningless in the case of Kingstown. This was a national issue of poor survey design.

The 1901 census was conducted less than a year after the Browne report. Browne's report covers the missing addresses. Censuses, properly conducted, are normally considered reliable sources of information, whereas Browne's survey was a one-off survey undertaken by a medical inspector and by staff working on his team. We have to believe that Browne recorded what he saw. It is not credible to suggest that he invented some addresses. The addresses missing from the census did exist, and this can be verified by reference to other sources. So why are so many of them missing from the census? Possible explanations include:

- Unwillingness to enter – The census-takers were the local police constables. They would have had good excuses for not entering the courts and laneways. At the most basic level, the courts were unhygienic, filthy, smelly, and disease-prone. Taking census details in such an environment would have been an unpleasant task.
- Hostile environment – The police would likely have been unwelcome in the courts where their normal function was the enforcement of law and the apprehension of criminals.
- Relevance – Little consideration was given to the poor in the operation and administration of the town. They could not vote. They made little difference to the economic, social, and cultural life within the town and they were considered irrelevant. For that reason, it is possible that little effort was made to ensure their inclusion.
- Awareness – Throughout all reports on the town, there are references to the hidden nature of poverty. It was hidden in backyards, in cul-de-sacs entered through doorways and arches. It is understandable that some of these places could easily be missed.
- Political consideration – Kingstown had a bad record of care for the poor in terms of social housing, disease prevention, and so on. Many parties concerned with the administration of the town, such as those associated with the tourism business, may have had an interest in concealing the true statistics.

The following table shows addresses included in Browne's report but not listed in the census. In preparing this list, we have attempted to remove all situations of doubt, such as where different spellings of the same address might be used, as in Burn's Court or Byrne's Court, or different variants, as in Long's Row and Long's Lane. The column marked 'Number of dwellings' is the number as reported by Browne.

The total number of dwellings on this list is 203. This figure is almost certainly an underestimate of the number omitted from the 1901 census. There are many cases where addresses were shown in the census, but with a much smaller number of dwellings than in the Browne report. If we assume an occupancy rate of four people per dwelling, then we can assume that over 1,000 people from the poorer classes were omitted from the census.

Address	Number of dwellings	Address	Number of dwellings
Archbold's Court	4	Finnegan's Court	4
Avoca Square AKA Ovoca Square	18	Finnegan's Court (2)	10
Beatty's Court	9	Fitzhenry's Court	4
Bond's Court	10	Knight's Cottages AKA Knight's Court	3
Brazil's Court	3	Larkin's Yard	8
Bruce's Court	7	Lerinimon's Court	7
Carroll's Court	3	Marlow's Court AKA Marlow's Place	8
Carroll's Court	5	Mc Cormack's Court	3
Chandler's Court	24	Mooney's Court	5
Clancy's Court	4	Penston's Court	3
Connolly's Court	7	Reid's Court	4
Cunningham's Court	5	Synott's Court	5
Dolan's Court	7	Tierney's Court	7
Dowling's Court	3	Toomey's Court	5
Eubank's Court	7	White's Court (2)	5
Eubank's Court(2)	6		

HOUSE TYPES

The 1901 census shows 418 third-class dwellings and no fourth-class dwellings. All other houses are classified as second class or first class.

The Browne survey lists '1,007 houses of the poorer class'. He describes them as 'a considerable proportion are barely fit for habitation and many are quite unfit'. This would certainly suggest that in any reasonable classification of dwellings on a scale of 1 to 4, most or all of them should be classified as third or fourth class.

This apparent mismatch is explained by the points system used in the census, which was as follows:

Feature	Points allocated
Walls	1 point if walls are stone, brick, or concrete
Roof	1 point if roof is slated, tiled, or made of iron
Rooms	1 point for a 1-room house 2 points for a 2, 3, or 4 room house 3 points for a 5 or 6 room house 4 points for a 7, 8, or 9 room house 5 points for a 10, 11, or 12 room house 6 points for a 13 or more room house
Windows in front	1 point for every window in the front of the house

The total number of points provided a classification as follows:

First-class house	Second-class house	Third-class house	Fourth-class house
12 points or more	6 to 11 points	3 to 5 points	1 or 2 points

This points system meant that any house was at least a third-class house if it had a solid roof and solid walls. The lean-to dwellings within the courts had solid walls and roofs. If they had two windows or two rooms, they were classified as second class. The classification of fourth class only applied to tents, caves, thatched buildings, or mud-wall buildings.

In summary, the classification arrangement in the census does not present a reasonable overview that might be of value to the historian.

THE KINGSTOWN IMPROVEMENT SCHEMES

WESTMINSTER PASSES THE HOUSING OF THE WORKING CLASSES ACT 1890

In 1890, the Westminster government introduced the Housing of the Working Classes Act 1890. It was intended to enable local authorities to create schemes to deal with the following:

Houses, courts, or alleys which were unfit for human habitation. The narrowness, closeness, and bad arrangement, or the bad condition of the streets and houses or groups of houses within such areas, or the want of light, air, ventilation, or proper conveniences, or any other sanitary defects, or one or more of such causes, are dangerous or injurious to the health of the inhabitants either of the buildings in the said area or of the neighbouring buildings; and that the evils connected with such houses, courts, or alleys, and the sanitary defects in such area cannot be effectually remedied otherwise than by an improvement scheme.

The act was one of the so-called public health acts of the period. It represented a major increase in State intervention and a change to the hitherto *laissez-faire* approach. Defective housing provided by unscrupulous landlords would be replaced by modern, clean accommodation provided by a local authority. Each scheme would have to be sanctioned by parliament. Each scheme would have to be self-financing, with rents sufficient to repay the funds borrowed for the cost of construction.

The title of the act, however, gave a clue to its intentions. It was intended to provide housing for those who had a job and an income sufficient to pay the required rent. It was not intended for those in real poverty or for the unemployed.

THE URBAN DISTRICT COUNCIL AND HOUSING OF THE POOR

The most widely used word in the minutes of the Urban District Council, in health-related legislation and in the courts, is the word 'nuisance'. In the council minutes, the term 'nuisance' invariably refers to complaints received by the council in relation to the hygiene of the town and specifically to faulty sewers or unclean courts, lanes, and areas occupied by the poorer classes. The Number One Committee of the Urban District Council was the one that dealt with nuisances among other items. Each meeting started with long lists of nuisances, either attended to or pending.

In a report for the year 1900, submitted to the Council in May 1901, the sanitary officer, J. Byrne Power, was rather sanguine about the situation. In a paragraph on 'The Dwellings of the Poor' he reported:

It is easy to convince the public of the great evil that exists, but, unfortunately, it seems very difficult to apply an effectual remedy. Yet, it is most desirable that the utmost efforts should be made, as upon the solution of the problem depends most assuredly our advance as a sea-side health resort. In dealing with this matter, there is one point that must never be lost sight of – that is the fact that wretched and miserable as is the condition of those dwellings in Kingstown, yet they have one great advantage over those in all cities and in some other Urban Districts. I allude to the fact that they are nearly all one-storied cabins. This circumstance, and this alone, prevents those hovels being the hotbeds of infectious disease to the same extent as are the tenement houses, of many storeys, in other places, where the poor are huddled away out of sight and out of ken. It is, therefore, to be hoped that when these cabins are demolished, they will be replaced by one-storied cottages.

Later in the same report, the sanitary officer seemed to say that the solutions to the problem were within the realms of finance, and were not within his domain. He did not seem to get much support for this view.

Within the next two years, however, the matter had moved from being a sanitation issue to being an issue for cooperation between many departments of the council to develop and manage the Kingstown Improvement Scheme 1902. A Housing of Working Classes Committee had been formed within the Council and was meeting on a regular basis, frequently more than once per week.

While all this was happening, the Browne report was published in 1902. If the government needed any assurance of the need for a scheme for Kingstown, they only had to look to that report. Kingstown/Dún Laoghaire certainly met the criteria for a scheme under multiple headings.

By January 1903, the Urban District Council was able to recommend schemes for:

- The accommodation of twenty-two families on Tivoli Terrace in separate two-storey houses.
- The arrangement of the remainder of that plot in streets 9m (30ft) wide with rows of two-storey houses, 6m (20ft) apart, with one family on the ground floor, and another family on the upper floor with a separate entrance from the street. These would provide ninety-six habitations with living room, two bedrooms, WC, and scullery on Wolfe Tone Avenue and Desmond Avenue.
- The construction, on the other side of Cross Avenue, of housing for thirteen families.
- The housing of a further eighty-four families on the remainder of the site.

A month later, the committee was looking at various plans for the Cumberland Street site and sites at Sallynoggin.

In a letter dated April 1903, the Local Government Board broadly supported the schemes and indicated that specific authorisation would be provided under the Housing of the Working Classes Act 1890. An enabling act, called the Housing of the Working Classes Act (Ireland) 1903, was passed later that year.

SPECIFIC LEGISLATION FOR KINGSTOWN AND ATHLONE

To enact a scheme of this type, it was necessary to pass authorising legislation at Westminster. A new act called the Housing of the Working Classes (Ireland) Act 1903 was in the course of preparation, but it appears that the authorisation was in fact granted under the 1890 act. When the specific authorising legislation, known as 'A Bill to Confirm certain Provisional Orders of the Local Government Board for Ireland relating to the Urban Districts of Athlone and Kingstown', was prepared in 1903, the term 'labouring classes' was used instead of 'working class'. It appears that the government considered that too many civil servants were availing of housing under the early schemes. The expression 'labouring class' was defined as:

- Mechanics, artisans, labourers, and others working for wages.
- Hawkers, costermongers, persons not working for wages but working at some trade or handicraft without employing others except members of their own families.
- Persons other than domestic servants whose income does not exceed an average of 30 shillings a week.
- The families of any such persons who may be residing with them.

The appendix to the bill provides details of the courts to be demolished to facilitate the new development:

Part one dealt with the following addresses: Molloy's Court, Clark's Court, Kelly's Court, Sexton's Court, Hilton's Court, Byrne's Court, Cumberland Street, and York Street. This was referred to as the 'unhealthy area'. The cost of clearing these sites would be £6,600, and the cost of new buildings would be £16,000. This section enabled the construction of brick-fronted houses in Cumberland Street, Barrett Street, and parts of Smyth's Villas. In fact, by the time it was sanctioned, the scheme was already under way.

Part two enabled the compulsory acquisition of various courts and other defective houses. The list included some houses at Cross Avenue, Turner's Avenue, Larkin's Yard, Bond's Court, Long's Row, Mooney's Court, Tivoli Avenue, Ard's Court, Paradise Row, Bryan's Court, Hassard's Court, Gannon's Court, Ruth's Court, Toole's Court, Northcote Avenue, and Courtney's Cottages. This section enabled the clearance for construction of houses in Wolfe Tone Avenue, Desmond Avenue, Cross Avenue, Dominick Street, and Convent Road.

The scheme included a clause that required that the new houses should be put in place and made fit for occupation before the old houses were removed.

There are a number of interesting things about the order that sanctioned the schemes. In part two, the properties are listed individually. The owners are recorded as being Lords Longford and de Vesci, but with various intermediaries acting as lessors. We have to believe that both the landlords and the intermediaries shared the small rents paid by the occupiers of these dwellings. The name of each occupier is also listed in the government order.

Many of the dwellings in these areas were back-to-back, or otherwise arranged in groups. In such cases, it lists the combined site area in square perches. The site areas were very small.

By far the biggest example is that of Hassard's Court, in the area where Dominick Street now stands. It shows twenty dwellings in a site measuring 1 rood, 36 perches, 10 square yards, which equates to less than half an acre, including roadway and backyards.

Certain houses on Cross Avenue backed on to Gannon's Court. This combined group of eighteen houses shared a yard. The total area for the eighteen houses, including the yard and roadways, was less than a quarter of an acre. By any reasonable standards, this is an extraordinary and unacceptable level of housing density.

The table on this page lists municipal housing in Kingstown and Dún Laoghaire from 1904 to 1936 (extracted from 'Dún Laoghaire – its history, scenery and development' prepared for Dún Laoghaire Borough Corporation by Manning Robertson in 1936).

Scheme	Location	Number of houses	Number of flats	Date
Cross Avenue Area	Dún Laoghaire	38	191	1904
Barrett Street	Dún Laoghaire	56		1905
Glasthule Buildings	Dún Laoghaire		75	1908
Northcote Avenue	Dún Laoghaire	6		1912
Library Road	Dún Laoghaire	12		1912
Bentley Villas	Dún Laoghaire	10		1923
Kelly's Villas	Dún Laoghaire	5		1923
St Brendan's Terrace	Dún Laoghaire	8		1932
St Michael's Terrace	Dún Laoghaire	8		1932
Smyth's Villas	Dún Laoghaire	14		1934
Hybla	Dún Laoghaire	25		1935
York Road	Dún Laoghaire	40		1935
Devitt Villas	Glasthule	25		1923
O'Donnell Gardens	Glasthule	46		1930
Congress Gardens	Glasthule	37		1932
Eden Villas	Glasthule	101		1934
Dixon's Villas	Glasthule	16		1934
Carriglea Gardens	Kill Avenue	56		1932
Sarsfield Street	Sallynoggin	40		1911–12
Main Street	Sallynoggin	10		1911–12
Mary Street	Sallynoggin	26		1912
Emmett Street	Sallynoggin	7		1918
Parnell Street	Sallynoggin	29		1918
Sallynoggin Villas	Sallynoggin	20		1923
Sallynoggin	Sallynoggin	81		1935–36
Monkstown Farm (under construction)	Monkstown	146		1936
Totals		862	266	

HOUSES BUILT

Over the three years following the commencement of the scheme, 38 houses and 191 flats were built on Cross Avenue and the immediately surrounding streets. 'Flats' was the term used to describe houses constructed for sharing, where one family lived upstairs while another lived downstairs. A further fifty-six houses were built in the area of Barrett Street and Cumberland Street. All of these houses were finished in a dark-red brick and are a distinctive feature of the town today. Many of the flats have been modified internally so that they are now single-family dwellings.

TRANSITION AND AFTERWARDS

The Kingstown Improvement Scheme was developed on a promise that the residents of the older houses would not be displaced until the new houses were ready for occupation. Newspaper reports of the time say that the process did not run smoothly and these are confirmed by a 1907 medical officer report.

This 1907 report by the Medical Officer of Health to the Public Health Committee, published in the *Irish Independent* on 27 March 1907, stated that, in the period from 1881 to 1907, 628 houses were demolished. These houses had a population of about 2,085. There were still 826 dwellings with a population of 3,387. Some of this group were being rehoused in the new dwellings. The clearing away of most of the slums had caused the inhabitants to overcrowd into those that remained.

Over the succeeding three to four years, there were regular reports in the newspapers of meetings between the council and the legal representatives of the landlords. During these meetings, the council sought to force the landlords to do improvements to the remaining stock of smaller houses, but such attempts produced little improvement.

Over the subsequent years, a range of schemes of municipal houses were built around the town. In a 1936 planning report, Manning Robertson provided a table of those schemes and their completion dates.

MANNING ROBERTSON REPORT

In a 1936 report entitled 'Dún Laoghaire – its history, scenery and development', prepared for Dún Laoghaire Borough Corporation, Manning Robertson, a town-planning consultant, reviewed the history of municipal housing in the borough. Robertson was an Irish-born, English-educated architect who designed municipal housing for much of Monkstown Farm and Temple Hill, Blackrock.

The previous table, selected from the Robertson report, includes those municipal houses constructed in the town itself, and in the neighbouring areas of the borough, but excludes those in Blackrock, Killiney, and Dalkey.

By 1936, Robertson considered that 'Thanks to the efforts which have been made by the Corporation, the housing situation in Dún Laoghaire is unusually satisfactory'. It is likely that some of the citizens of the town would have disagreed.

STATISTICAL EXTRACTS FROM REPORTS

The following table shows statistical data collected from the four specified sources on various locations in Kingstown/Dún Laoghaire. We recognise that there are some problems with the data, and have made best endeavours to ensure correctness. In certain cases locations have similar but not identical names in two reports. In such cases we have made judgements based upon the other characteristics or information from other sources. We must also recognise that there are a number of cases where two or more separate locations have identical names, e.g. Sexton's Court, Dignam's Court.

Many locations appear in only one, two or three of the four reports from which these extracts were made.

GRIFFITHS VALUATION, 1849

Number of houses	This is the number of holdings at the location that have the word 'house' in the description
Number of houses <£2 19s 11d	Houses with a valuation under £3
Number of houses £3–£5	Houses with valuation in the range £3–£5
Haliday report 1867	The report by Charles Haliday and Thomas More Madden
Deficient houses	This is the term used by Haliday
Privy	How many privies in the location (these were normally shared between a number of households)
Ashpit	How many ashpits (for disposal of human waste) in the location (these were normally shared between a number of households)

BROWNE, 1900 (PUBLISHED 1902)

Number of houses	Number of houses in this location
WC, privy, ashpit, bin	Number of each type of facility for disposal of human waste (these were normally shared between a number of households)

CENSUS 1901

Number of houses	Number of houses at this location
Number of households	A household may include members of a family and their visitors, boarders, servants, etc. Each household submitted a Household Return (Form A). There was frequently more than one household in a house
Third-class houses	Houses were classified according to a crude points system – see the section on Census 1901 for details
Number overcrowded	Defined by us for the purposes of this report as houses having more than two persons per room e.g. three people or more in a one-room house, five people or more in a two-room house etc.

Address	Griffith's Valuation 1849			Haliday 1867			Browne 1900					Census 1901			
	Number of houses	Number of houses <£2 19s 11d	Number of houses £3–£5	No. of deficient houses	Privy	Ashpit	No. of houses	WC	Privy	Ashpit	Bin	No. of houses	No. of households	No. of third-class houses	Number overcrowded
Adelaide Place	2	0	0												
Adelaide Street	20	0	0									26	47	0	0
Air Hill Avenue	3	0	0												
Albert Place	19	0	16	24	1	1	26	1	5	5		23	28	2	8
Albert Terrace	5	0	0										3	0	0
Andersons Court	2	0	2												
Andrews Court				3	1	1						2	2	0	1
Anglesea Cottages							11	3			2	9	14	4	1
Archbold's Court	3	2	0	3	0	1	4	1			1				
Arde's Court AKA Airds Court AKA Arde's Cottages	2	2	0				6	1		1		5	5	3	0
Ardnagreina												3	5	0	0
Atwell's Court AKA Atwool's Court	2	2	0				10	1		1		6	6	6	2
Avoca Square AKA Ovoca Square							18	1			1				
Avondale												7	8	1	3
Back Road	26	3	2												
Balls Court				8	1	1						5	5	1	2
Baxters Court				4	1	1	5	2			2	4	4	0	1
Baxters Lane												3	5		1
Baylis Court	2	0	2												
Baymount Court				20	0	1									
Beatty's Court							9	1		1					
Beaumont Place	5	3	2												
Begg's Court							8	2			2				
Beggs Lane												5	9	7	
Bond's Cottages							8		1	1					
Bond's Court				15	1	1	10	1			1				
Bond's Lane	7	7	0									13	13	13	8
Boyd's Court							4		1	1					
Boyles Court															
Bradley's Lane AKA Bradleys Court	6	3	3	7	1	1									
Brazil's Court							3	1			1				

Address	Griffith's Valuation 1849			Haliday 1867			Browne 1900					Census 1901			
	Number of houses	Number of houses <£2 19s 11d	Number of houses £3–£5	No. of deficient houses	Privy	Ashpit	No. of houses	WC	Privy	Ashpit	Bin	No. of houses	No. of households	No. of third-class houses	Number overcrowded
Brewsters Cottages							10					7	7	4	6
Brian's Court							10	2			2				
Brian's Court (2)							9		1	1					
Brien's Court												7	7	7	5
Bruce's Court				8	2	1	7	1			1				
Bryans Court												7	7	1	5
Burnes Court AKA Byrnes Court				6	1	1	6	1			1	3	4	1	2
Byrne's cottages							5	1		1		5	5	1	2
Byrne's Court	7	7	0	8	1	1						9	9	9	
Byrne's Court	4	3	1				14	1			1	4	4	1	6
Byrne's Court							4	1			1				
Byrne's Court				12	1	1									
Byrne's Land	7	7	0												
Callaghan's Lane	15	4	6	9	1	1						25	29	21	19
Cambridge Place												3	6	0	1
Carlisle Terrace												6	6	0	0
Carrig Court	4	2	1												
Carroll's Cottages							24	3	3	3					
Carroll's Court				7	2	2	3		1	1					
Carroll's Court							5	1			1				
Castella Place	10	0	10												
Chandler's Court				2	0	0	24	3			3				
Charlemont Avenue												11	15	0	1
Charlemont Terrace	13	0	1									6	6	0	0
Clancy's Court							4	1			2				
Clarence Place				19	2	1						4	4	3	0
Clarence Street	22	0	6	2	0	1						9	18	0	6
Clarinda Park East												51	67	0	0
Clarinda Park North												14	23	0	0
Clarinda Park West												38	45	0	0
Clarke's Court							7	2			1	5	5	5	0
Clarke's Court				11	1	1	6	1			1				
Clock Lane	10	0	0									15	25	2	1
Coal Quay												1	1	0	0
Codd's Lane	5	0	0	13	0	0									

Address	Griffith's Valuation 1849			Haliday 1867			Browne 1900					Census 1901			
	Number of houses	Number of houses <£2 19s 11d	Number of houses £3–£5	No. of deficient houses	Privy	Ashpit	No. of houses	WC	Privy	Ashpit	Bin	No. of houses	No. of households	No. of third-class houses	Number overcrowded
Cody's Court	5	5	0	5	1	1						5	5	5	1
Connaught Terrace AKA Connaught Place	5	0	0									3	5	0	0
Connolly's Court							7	1			1				
Connor's Court(1)	9	9	0									4	4	3	0
Connor's Court(2)							5	1			1	4	4	0	1
Corrig Avenue	19	0	0									34	35	1	0
Corrig Castle												2	2	1	0
Corrig Castle Terrace	5	1	0										2	0	0
Crimmins Court												5	5	0	4
Crofton Avenue												12	25	0	5
Crofton Parade												11	11	11	4
Crofton Parade				6	2	1	12	1			1				
Crofton Place												1	1	0	0
Crofton Road												12	12	1	0
Crofton Terrace	7	0	0									7	8	1	0
Cromer's Court	3	3	0												1
Cross Avenue				21	0	1						58	62	12	25
Crosthwaite Park East												14	14	0	0
Crosthwaite Park South												11	11	0	0
Crosthwaite Park West												16	16	0	0
Crosthwaite Terrace												2	2	0	0
Cumberland Street	31	0	3									29	45	15	6
Cummin's Court							4	1			1	3	3	3	3
Cunningham's Court							5	1			1				
Darby's Court	8	4	4												6
Darcy's Court				5	2	1									
De Vesci Place	10	0	0									2	2	0	
De Vesci Terrace (including Sloperton)	16	0	0									14	14	0	0
Delany's Court	7	7	0	8	1	1									
Diamond Place				4	1	1	10	2		1		8	8	0	2
Dignam's Court (2)							7	1			1				
Dignan's Court AKA Dignams Court or Digmans Court	5	5	0	5	1	1	6	1			1	5	5	5	2

Address	Griffith's Valuation 1849			Haliday 1867			Browne 1900					Census 1901			
	Number of houses	Number of houses <£2 19s 11d	Number of houses £3–£5	No. of deficient houses	Privy	Ashpit	No. of houses	WC	Privy	Ashpit	Bin	No. of houses	No. of households	No. of third-class houses	Number overcrowded
Dixon's Cottages							8		1	1					
Dockrell's Court				4	1	1									
Dolan's Court							7	1			1				
Dowling's Court							3	1			1				
Doyle's Court	13	12	1												
Doyle's Lane				4	1	1									
Duffs Court				3	1	1						6	6	3	4
Duff's Court (2)												5	5	0	3
Durham Place												4	6	0	1
East Pier												4	4	2	0
Eblana Avenue												8	10	0	0
Eglington Park												12	12	0	
Eldens Court + battery East Pier												3	3	0	0
Eldon's Court							5	1			1				
Eubank's Court							7	1			2				
Eubank's Court (2)							6	1			2				
Evan's Court	5	5	0												
Fagan's Court												5	5	3	3
Finnegan's Court				4	1	1	4	1			1				
Finnegan's Court (2)				8	1	1	10	2			2				
Fitzhenry's Court							4		1	1					
Fitzpatrick's Court				12	1	1	12	1			1	9	10	9	5
Flanagan's Court no 1	4	3	1									4	4	3	3
Flanagan's Court no 2	5	1	4												
Flynn's Court	5	5	0				4		1	1		2	2	1	1
Foley's Court	4	4	0	3	1	1									
Foster's Court	6	2	3	3	1	1	5	1			1	5	5	3	2
Foster's Court							10	1		1					
Foster's Place												5	5	0	4
Gannon's Row aka Gannons Court	4	4	0	9	1	1	10		1	1		10	10	10	5
Garvy's Court				8	1	1									
George's Place	15		0									16	32	0	1
Gibraltar Place	3	0	0									3	3	1	1
Glenageary Road	2	0	1									12	12	1	2

Address	Griffith's Valuation 1849			Haliday 1867			Browne 1900					Census 1901			
	Number of houses	Number of houses <£2 19s 11d	Number of houses £3–£5	No. of deficient houses	Privy	Ashpit	No. of houses	WC	Privy	Ashpit	Bin	No. of houses	No. of households	No. of third-class houses	Number overcrowded
Goat Alley	10	4	5												
Goff's Court				21	0	2									
Gough's Court												2	2	2	1
Gresham Terrace	11	0	0									9	9	0	1
Gresham Lane												3	4	0	1
Haddington Terrace	12	0	0									9	10	0	0
Haigh's Terrace	7	0	0									6	9	0	0
Hall's Court	8	8	0				3	1			1	2	2	0	0
Hanlon's Court							10	1			1	7	7	0	3
Hassard's Court AKA Echo Court AKA Acho Court	24	17	6	24	2	1	24	2		1		25	25	25	20
Healy's Court	2	0	0												
Hilton's Court							11	1			1	6	8	2	1
Hogan's Court				6	1	1									
Hope Court	4	2	2												
Howard Place												2	2	0	0
Hyne's Court	4	0	4												
Jennings Court				4	1	1									
Jones's Court	3	3	0	3	0	1	8	2			1	4	5	2	3
Kelly's Avenue	17	2	4	3	1	1						20	24	5	11
Kelly's Court	20	20		13	3	3	10	2			2	10	10	2	7
Kingstown Avenue	97	2	94	17	3	3						65	88	13	25
Kinsella's Court				5	1	1									
Knight's Cottages AKA Knights Court				3	1	2	3	1			1				
Laceys Court AKA Lacy's Court				5	1	1	4	1			1	2	2	0	1
Larkin's Yard							8	1		1					
Lerinimon's Court							7	1			1				
Longford Terrace East	6	0	0									4	4	0	0
Long's Row	9	7	2				6		2	2					0
Lower Georges Street	138	3	8									97	145	21	13
Lowry's Court	2	1	1												
Lyburns Cottages												8	8	8	4
Maher's Court				4	1	1						2	2	1	1
Marine Terrace	11	0	0									9	9	0	0

Address	Griffith's Valuation 1849			Haliday 1867			Browne 1900					Census 1901			
	Number of houses	Number of houses <£2 19s 11d	Number of houses £3–£5	No. of deficient houses	Privy	Ashpit	No. of houses	WC	Privy	Ashpit	Bin	No. of houses	No. of households	No. of third-class houses	Number overcrowded
Marlow's Court AKA Marlow's Place	8	7	1	8	1	1	8	1			1				0
Mar's Court or Mars Court	5	3	2												
Martin's Court				2	1	1	2	2		1		3	3	0	1
Matthew Terrace												3	3	0	0
Mc Cormack's Court	3	2	1				3	1		1					
McCormick's Court				24	1	1									
McEntee's Court				4	1	1									
McGillick Court							4	1		1		4	4	2	1
Meledy's Court	2	2	0												0
Mellifont Avenue	20	0	0									24	47	0	0
Milliken's Court	10	4	4	11	1	1	11	1			1	12	14	6	5
Milliken's Court (2)				6	1	1									
Molloy's Court				5	1	1	4	1			1	3	3	3	3
Mooney's Court							5	1			1				
Moran's Court							4		1	1		3	3	2	1
Mosaphir Terrace												5	5	0	0
Mulgrave Place	5	0	0												
Mulgrave Terrace	10	0	10									20	29	0	1
Mullady's Court	2	1	1												
Murphy's Court	7	4	3	7	1	1	4	1			1	3	4	3	3
Murphy's Lane												1	1	0	0
Murray's Court	3	3	0												
Murtagh's Court no 1	2	1	1												
Murtagh's Court no 2	3	3	0												
Needham's Court	3	3	0	13	2	2	14	1			2	8	8	8	1
Northcote Avenue	4	0	0	3	0	0						35	34	5	16
Northumberland Avenue	49	0	0									42	79	0	0
Northumberland Place	2	0	0									3	5	0	0
Nugents Court				5	1	1	5	1			1	3	3	0	1
Nulty's Court				5	0	0						6	6	0	1
O'Brien's Court	3	2	1												
O'Carroll's Court No 1	8	8	0									1	1	1	1
O'Carroll's Court No. 2	4	4	0												
Old Dun Leary	20	2	2									5	7	1	2

Address	Griffith's Valuation 1849			Haliday 1867			Browne 1900					Census 1901			
	Number of houses	Number of houses <£2 19s 11d	Number of houses £3–£5	No. of deficient houses	Privy	Ashpit	No. of houses	WC	Privy	Ashpit	Bin	No. of houses	No. of households	No. of third-class houses	Number overcrowded
Old Dunleary Road	8	0	6												2
Paradise Place				8	0	0									
Paradise Row – 1849															
Paradise Row 1900	22	2	7									18	24	4	13
Pave Lane AKA Paved Lane				18	2	4	7	2			2	6	6	5	2
Penston's Court							3	1			1				
Pims Court							19	3			3	11	11	10	5
Quay or Harbour Road												1	1	0	0
Quay Road												7	7	0	1
Reid's Court				5	1	1	4	1			1				
Roberts' Court AKA Robinsons Court				4	1	0									
Roby Place	4	0	0									4	4	0	0
Rogan's Court				8	1	1	8	1			1	7	7	7	7
Royal Marine Road												8	10	0	0
Royal Terrace East												15	15	0	0
Royal Terrace North												1	1	0	0
Royal Terrace West												30	30	0	0
Rumley Avenue AKA Mulgrave Street	58	0	3	8	1	1						67	151	17	33
Ryan's Court				10	1	1						8	8	1	4
Seaview Terrace												4	4	1	2
Sextons Court (Clarence Street)							4	1			1	19	23	0	17
Sexton's Court (Lr Georges Street)							8	1			1				
Sextons Court (Cumberland Street)				4	1	1	5	1			1	5	5	5	3
Sextons Court (York Street)												1	1	0	
Sharkey's Court	4	4	0				6	1			1	3	3	3	2
Stable Lane	2	0	1												
Stable Lane	1		0	1	0	0									
Stable Lane	1	0	1												
Stephen's Court	4	4	0	7	1	1	6	1			1	5	5	5	0
Stoneview Place	18	1	0	15	4	4	20		5	5		17	27	2	10
Susan Place	15	4	2									3	3	0	1
Sussex Parade	8	0	0												

Address	Griffith's Valuation 1849			Haliday 1867			Browne 1900					Census 1901			
	Number of houses	Number of houses <£2 19s 11d	Number of houses £3–£5	No. of deficient houses	Privy	Ashpit	No. of houses	WC	Privy	Ashpit	Bin	No. of houses	No. of households	No. of third-class houses	Number overcrowded
Sussex Street	11	0	0									14	24	0	0
Sword's Court	3	2	1	4	1	1	4		1	1		2	2	1	1
Synnott Terrace												7	7	0	3
Synnott's Court							3	1			1	2	2	1	1
Synott's Court							5	1			1				
Tierney's Court							7	1			1				
Tinch's Court	2	2	0												
Tivoli Avenue	25	7	16	22	3	3						22	23	15	18
Tivoli Parade												2	2	0	0
Tivoli Place												7	12	0	2
Tivoli Road												2	7	0	0
Tivoli Terrace	16	0	0												
Tivoli Terrace East	17	0	1									21	27	0	2
Tivoli Terrace North												22	38	0	0
Tivoli Terrace South												14	15	0	0
Tooles Court				4	0	0	3	1			1	4	4	4	4
Tooles Court (2)				4	0	0									
Toomey's Court							5	1			1				
Turners Avenue												26	26	25	18
Turner's Lane AKA Paradise Place	16	9	4												2
Upper George's Street	83	0	0									87	110	3	6
Valetta Avenue												2	2	0	0
Victoria Terrace	3	0	0									1	1	0	0
Walch's Court				5	1	1									
Walnut's Court	7	7	0												0
Wellington Place	16	2	0				9	2			2	6	6	0	5
Wellington Street				5	1	2						20	38	1	7
West Pier												1	1	0	1
White's Court (1)	5	4	1	8	1	1	6	2		1		5	5	4	2
White's Court (2)				6	1	1	5		1	1					
White's Court				4	1	1									
William's Court AKA Williams Cottages							7	1			1	7	7	3	5
York Street	72	0	5									24	29	4	3
York Terrace	5	0	0									4	8	0	2